Marriage is a bumpy and twisting road for every couple. Add chronic illness issues to the mix and the challenges multiply, but so, too, the rewards. As we worked our way through each chapter, while we often found ourselves weeping, we were also encouraged, drawn closer to our glorious God and to His specific purposes for our lives. If chronic illness is a reality for you or a loved one, this is a must-read.

KARIN FENDICK, author of *From Ashes to Glory: A Psalm a Day*

I Take You In Sickness & In Health: Marriage with Chronic Illness offers insight into how to improve commitment, understanding and communication while living with a spouse who lives with chronic pain. Throughout this book you are led to God's Word through Bible verses that provide wisdom, strength, patience and comfort to face each day together.

RICHARD and CHRISTINE FELDSCHNEIDER

You have done a wonderful job, and many chronic illness couples can benefit from reading and applying the Scripture, activities, and experience you share. My husband and I have been married 34 years and I've had chronic pain nearly 26 years. Reading *I Take You In Sickness & In Health: Marriage with Chronic Illness*, I recognized stages and issues we'd worked through over time. I wish this book had been available years ago. We found our way, thank the Lord, but this resource will now help other married couples who are dealing with chronic illness. Thank you for your ministry to others! May the Lord continue to bless you, your marriage and family, this book, and those who will read it.

KRIS HANSSON ROBINSON

When you or your spouse becomes chronically ill, nothing really prepares you for how that might change your marriage. This is a very real, candid and open way of looking at how to keep your marriage vibrant, alive and possibly part of your healing. A great book for any couple to go through!

SANDIE LOVREIN

Chronic Joy Ministry has been a light in the dark places that we have had to travel through diagnosis after diagnosis. *I Take You In Sickness & In Health: Marriage with Chronic Illness* encourages couples on this journey. We have been encouraged, inspired, and empowered to reconnect as husband and wife, not just as caregiver and care-receiver. It is a needed and welcomed resource for any couple walking *together* through a marriage touched by chronic illness.

RANDY and GINA WEEKS

This book is a true blessing for all those who read it. Cindee, your gift to write and touch people in the midst of pain and hardship brings hope, love, and a remarkable new vision, a new beginning in our relationships with God and with our spouse. Thank you for sharing your gift with the world, and thank you to your family for sharing parts of their stories too.

HEIDI PETERSON, BSN

This is exceptional material for couples, Cindee. Thank you for pushing on even in your circumstances.

DIANE McELWAIN

I TAKE YOU IN SICKNESS & IN HEALTH
MARRIAGE WITH CHRONIC ILLNESS

©2018 by Cindee Snider Re
Published by Chronic Joy Ministry, Inc. Waukesha, WI 53188
chronic-joy.org

You are welcome to share portions of this book (in your book, on your blog,
in a classroom or small group, in a business or conference setting) without asking permission. We simply
ask that you cite Chronic Joy Ministry, Inc. and link back
to us at chronic-joy.org. That's it! Thanks for sharing!

First Edition: September, 2018
Printed in the United States of America
ISBN: 978-0-9978099-7-8

Unless otherwise noted, all Scripture is from the HOLY BIBLE, NEW INTERNATIONAL VERSION. © 1973, 1978, 1984 by International Bible Society. Used by permission of Zondervan. All rights reserved.

Cover Image and Interior Design: **kylecreative.com**
Author Photo: **Wayde Peronto** of **Babboni Photography**

End-of-Chapter Prayers: Tony Re

Printed by CreateSpace

Chronic Joy Ministry, Inc.
Radical hope. Compassionate change.
Equipping those affected by chronic physical and mental illness
through community and education rooted in Jesus Christ

I TAKE YOU IN SICKNESS & IN HEALTH
MARRIAGE WITH CHRONIC ILLNESS

Cindee Snider Re

Chronic Joy Ministry, Inc.
Waukesha, Wisconsin

This book is lovingly dedicated to so many who have loved one another *for a lifetime*:

My parents: *Don and Susie Snider*
My in-laws: *Tony and Ruth Re*

My grandparents:
Herbert and Mildred Moser
Wilson and Janet Snider

Others we love:

Roy & Millie Daikawa   *Karl & Dottie Schimpf*
Pete & Barb Rockaway   *Tom & Sue Campbell*
Mark & Ann Snider   *Dan & Judy Klotz*
Bill & Carmella Austin   *Mike & Mary Juneau*
Jerry & Sharon Mahoney   *Jeff and Deb Moll*

To my husband *Tony*, the man I love most in this world.

**And to *Kyle, Sam, Sarah, Anna & Megan*:
May you one day discover your own *love for a lifetime*.**

What greater thing is there for two human souls, than to feel that they are joined for life – to strengthen each other in all labor, to rest on each other in all sorrow, to minister to each other in all pain, to be one with each other in silent unspeakable memories at the moment of last parting.

George Eliot

Dear Heavenly Father

As we embark on this journey ahead, open our hearts and minds to the words on these pages and the conversations we will have with You and with our spouse.

We can be so guarded and careful because of past hurts, fears, doubts and worries. Give us the peace, strength and resolve to see beyond these and the courage to be humble and truthful in the words we write and speak.

Show us the hope, peace and joy that can come as we open our hearts to You and learn to trust You a little more each day.

In Jesus' name, amen.

Tony Re
Christ follower, husband, father, son, brother, caretaker, provider

*Let no debt remain outstanding,
except the continuing debt
to love one another ...
Romans 13:8*

Chronic Joy Ministry, Inc.

Chronic Joy Ministry, Inc. was founded to raise awareness of the nearly 1 in 2 people who live with chronic physical and mental illness and its impact on every aspect of life — faith, family, finances, friendships, marriage, education, hobbies and work.

Chronic illness *is* hard, but there *is hope*.

On January 1, 2016, I woke with a vision too big to believe. God broke my heart for the millions — yes, *millions!* — of people living daily with chronic illness, and also for the *one* utterly without hope.

In April 2016, we officially became a 501(c)(3) nonprofit, no small accomplishment. But God was just getting started.

Today, Chronic Joy Ministry offers daily encouragement across social media, has a growing website filled with educational resources and weekly guest blogs, publishes a monthly *Invitation to Prayer* and a quarterly *Invitation to Community*, and has published the first two books in our four-book Thrive study series as well as *Grace, Truth & Time*, our facilitator's guide.

Chronic Joy is a ministry led by God and His word. Luke 15:8-9 speaks to our purpose:

> Or suppose a woman has ten silver coins and loses one. Doesn't she light a lamp, sweep the house and search carefully until she finds it? And when she finds it, she calls her friends and neighbors together and says, "Rejoice with me; I have found my lost coin."

This woman had *hope* that she would find her lost coin. She had *purpose* as she searched for what was lost. From the beginning, she knew the intrinsic *worth* of a single coin. And when she found her one lost coin, she experienced such *joy*.

Those are the first four books in our study series: *Discovering Hope, Finding Purpose, Embracing Worth* and *Encountering Joy*. But they are more than titles — they are an invitation to live life with our eyes focused on God, for when we choose Him, He will compassionately change our hearts and lead us to radical hope, rediscovered purpose, eternal worth, and exquisite joy.

Pamela K. Piquette
President and Co-Founder, Chronic Joy Ministry, Inc.

PAMELA is a leader and a visionary following God's call to inspire those affected by chronic illness to discover hope, find purpose, embrace worth and encounter joy. She believes every precious life affected by chronic illness is both vital and purposed.

Pamela is a mom of three adult children, a grandma of two sweet granddaughters, and a wife of more than 30 years. She is diagnosed with Ehlers-Danlos Syndrome, chronic migraines and host of other chronic conditions.

Pamela enjoys hot tea, reading — almost always more than one book at a time — and walking her teddy bear dog, Cocoa.

Contents

Foreword *by Sheila Lagrand*	v
Introduction	1
1. Kindness	5
2. Growth	17
3. Willingness	27
4. Forgiveness	37
5. Time	49
6. Intimacy	69
7. Differences	81
8. Presence	95
9. Impact	109
10. Wellspring	121
Appendix	135
Small Group Policy	136
Small Group Contact Page	137
Build an Illness Ministry	139
Reproducible Prayer Request Cards	143
NIV Scripture Used in This Study	144
Cindee Snider Re	154
Acknowledgments	155
Discovering Hope	156
Finding Purpose	157
Embracing Worth	158
Encountering Joy	159
Grace, Truth & Time	160
Connect	161

*As God by creation made two of one,
so again by marriage, He made one of two.*
Thomas Adams

Foreword

My heart-sister Cindee Snider Re messaged me to tell me she had finished the manuscript for this book, "and your name keeps coming up in prayer to write the Foreword. Absolutely no pressure, but if you're interested, we'd love to have you."

I replied immediately, "I would love to! I am honored." And my words were true. I was honored. But I also felt unqualified. And angry. I felt unqualified because my health challenges — fibromyalgia, hypermobility syndrome, and what I've come to call my Baskin-Robbins back, as it has about 31 diagnoses — are not the kinds of illness that threaten my life. And somehow, somewhere, I embraced the lie that only life-threatening illnesses were serious. From that thought, I leapt to the logical error that if only life-threatening illnesses are serious, then my medical problems must be trivial. Surely somebody with a significant diagnosis would be a better choice to introduce this important book.

And yes, anger swelled, too. Since I defined my medical problems as insignificant, I should soldier on, toughen up, and refuse to adjust my lifestyle. I had flunked the stoicism test. The facts of our lives betrayed my failure to power through my health problems. My husband and I adopted big changes:

- In 2013, we sold our beloved boat, as an afternoon cruising the Pacific left my back cranky for days.
- I adopted shortcuts in the kitchen, even stooping to serving store-bought dinner rolls at our annual Thanksgiving feast.
- In 2017, we sold our home in our native California and relocated to Arizona, where we could manage without my full-time, professional salary.

Two points emerge from this short list of lifestyle changes. First, we may grieve losses that other folks would characterize as petty or even silly. So I couldn't serve my homemade, freshly baked dinner rolls on Thanksgiving anymore. How does that detail land on the same list as giving up a treasured pastime or moving away from one's lifelong home? When illness forces us to adjust our plans, we can reorganize with grace. Or, if you're like me, you can deny the pain and exhaustion and begrudge the changes that make life more bearable.

The second point underscores the need for this book. Notice I am discussing the facts of *our* lives and the big changes *we* adopted. Chronic illness affects our spouses. My husband has borne the changing limits of my capabilities with love, grace, encouragement, and good humor. When I watch him wash the dinner dishes or vacuum the living room, gratitude and guilt arm-wrestle in my heart. I intended to be his helpmeet.

Apparently, my plans for our future didn't quite align with God's plans for us.

A good friend once asked me, when I admitted that back pain had sidelined me for the day, "And what is the gift of that pain?" At the time I thought the question was crazy. But as Rich and I move through another year with no miracles sweeping away my symptoms, I begin to see the gifts.

My health challenges have led us to understand better the differences in our upbringing and worldviews. For example, I grew up in a household where "complaining" about pain was considered "whining." The unwritten, unassailable law went like this: If you need something, such as a glass of water, an aspirin, or a heating pad, then ask for it. Otherwise, exert some self-control and be quiet. Nobody wants to listen to you gripe about your aches and pains. Now, my husband's family accepted expressions of pain as a normal component of sickness. As you might imagine, these differences contributed to occasional bouts of marital conflict. My husband, drawing on his upbringing, assumed that if I was hurting I would let him know, and if I had not let him know, I must feel fine. Based on my childhood experiences, I assumed that since my husband knew my illnesses cause constant pain and fatigue, he should know I'm hurting and tired all the time. It took a few lively exchanges between us for me to understand that I need to open my mouth and tell my husband how I feel. For his part, Rich has learned to ask whether I am up to a walk through the mall or a dip in the pool. More importantly, God has given us both the eyes to see our real, flawed, vulnerable selves — and to cherish all of each other's characteristics.

If chronic illness is part of your household, I urge you to read this book and complete the exercises at the end of each chapter. God is with you in the middle of the pain and the hard and the crying out and the keeping quiet. Even in our suffering we remain His oaks of righteousness. *I Take You in Sickness & in Health: Marriage with Chronic Illness* shows us how to regain hope and joy as we negotiate the path through sickness.

> The Spirit of the Sovereign Lord is on me,
> because the Lord has anointed me
> to proclaim good news to the poor.
> He has sent me to bind up the brokenhearted,
> to proclaim freedom for the captives
> and release from darkness for the prisoners,
> to proclaim the year of the Lord's favor
> and the day of vengeance of our God,
> to comfort all who mourn,
> and provide for those who grieve in Zion—
> to bestow on them a crown of beauty
> instead of ashes,
> the oil of joy
> instead of mourning,
> and a garment of praise
> instead of a spirit of despair.
> They will be called oaks of righteousness,
> a planting of the Lord
> for the display of his splendor.
> **Isaiah 61:1-3**

Sheila Lagrand
Author of *Remembering for Ruth*

Grace is the currency of redemption and restoration.
Pastor Max Ramsey

Introduction

Marriage is exciting and thrilling and *hard*. Marriage with kids is precious and adventurous and *hard*. Marriage with four chronically ill kids is challenging and life changing and *hard*. Marriage with a chronically ill spouse is exhausting and stressful and messy and *hard*.

My husband Tony and I stepped into marriage as independent adults with growing careers. One at a time, we added five precious and very wanted children, who were, over the span of ten years, diagnosed with a genetic connective tissue disorder and myriad co-existing conditions.

As our medical files mushroomed, our marriage withered. Tony immersed himself in his growing career and I plunged headlong into medical competency, learning to coordinate specialized medical teams, tests, treatment plans, hospitalizations, medications, research studies, and insurance appeals.

Almost overnight, we inhabited two very different worlds. We weren't unfaithful and we didn't stray physically, but our priorities were suddenly at odds. We spoke different languages and held divergent goals. Our days were exhausting, tense, and strained, conversation was awkward and uncomfortable, and suddenly *nothing* was easy. It seemed as if every single thing in life had changed – what we did, where we went, how long we stayed, what we ate, where we slept, how we dressed, what we read, watched, listened to, shared, dreamed of, or even spent. Tony was living in a world the kids and I had abruptly left, a world with a one-way-only door. It felt as if we'd been plunged into wet cement. We were all just trying to survive.

For eight long years our marriage straddled this divide where the diagnoses piled up like a mudslide, and loved one began to question what I said, what we did, how we ate, how we lived. A few even accused me of making all this up and those relationships marooned like shipwrecks.

As the divide deepened, the kids and I felt increasingly isolated. Tony soldiered on. But we were all unhappy, staggering under illness' incessant and implacable weight.

When the waves first began to roll, Tony and I forgot to stand *together*. We forgot to reach for each other's hands the year my brother died and the year we lost his dad. We forgot when our middle daughter grew dangerously ill, and in the aftermath of a serious car accident. We forgot through those long nights of our son's illness, and as each of our daughters was diagnosed. We forgot as we cared for his mom and walked with my parents through systemic melanoma.

Yet as we stood at the breaking point, Tony and I realized we a choice – we could learn to lean together or continue to drift apart.

Our redemption story began the moment we admitted that we didn't really like each other anymore, didn't really know each other anymore. The rift between us was painful, dark and decades wide.

We had five kids in their teens and early 20s, four who were seriously ill, two who were scarred by self-harm, two who'd skimmed the edge of suicide, and one who was deep into addiction.

Yet against the odds, we were still married. Our kids were all *still here* – one family living under one roof. *That* was where we would begin.

Commitment *alone* was a daily victory, and it became our starting point, the foundation on which we would rebuild, and the story behind this book.

For despite the statistics and contrary to what we often felt, my husband and I were still committed to our marriage, and against all odds, we were committed to each other, to our kids, and to fighting for this listing, reeling, bone-weary and deeply wounded family.

We were both committed to finding each other again, but this time in God.

Photo: *Anna Grace Re Photography*

Love is patient, love is kind.
1 Corinthians 13:4a

Kindness 1

"Here," I grumbled to my husband as he hovered over my shoulder. "I'll stop what *I'm* doing so you can have my computer. I'll go take a shower."

"That is not love," I clearly heard in my heart as I walked down the hall.

"Yes, I know, Lord, and it's childish too," I silently shot back.

As the water washed over me, so did the words of **1 Corinthians 13**, mixed with a few of my own. "Love is patient. Love is kind." Love willingly steps aside so another can work, even if it's inconvenient.

Love "keeps no record of wrongs." It doesn't justify or rationalize or spin the truth, even when we fall short, even when it stings, even if the cost is steep.

Love doesn't compete or strive or step on others' toes, because Love accepts us *as we are*, all because of *who we are* – the crown of God's creation.

Love "is not rude, it is not self-seeking, it is not easily angered …" Love lays down his life for his friends.

Oh, Lord…

I wasn't asked to lay down my life. I was asked only for my computer *for a single hour*. If I can't patiently, kindly, willingly do even that, how could I ever lay down my life for another?

"... if I have faith that can move mountains, but have not love, I am nothing."

Those words, Lord! Not I *have* nothing, but I *am* nothing.

Without love, I am *nothing*.

I am Yours, Father, created in Your image, and You *are* love.

Without *You*, I am truly *nothing*.

Love "always protects, always trusts, always hopes, always perseveres. Love never fails."

STEPPING IN:

1. How many years have you been married?

2. How did you meet your husband/wife?

3. What characteristics first drew you to your spouse?

4. How do you feel in your marriage today?

   - content
   - frustrated
   - boring
   - angry
   - respectful
   - friendly
   - committed
   - caring
   - blessed
   - broken
   - painful
   - troubled
   - loyal
   - honest
   - safe
   - distant
   - other:

5. Read **1 Corinthians 13:2b-3** and fill in the blanks:

   … and if I have a _____ that can move _____, but have

   not _____, I am _____. If I give _____ I

   possess to the _____ and _____ my body to the

   flames, but have _____ _____, I _____

   nothing.

   We can give without love. There are generous examples of that kind of philanthropy nearly every day. But to give *in* love, *with* love, *through* love, and because *God is love*, that changes everything.

6. In a few sentences or bullet points, describe the love between you and your spouse today.

GOING DEEPER:

7. Are you frustrated, angry, agitated or hurt by your marriage relationship?

When do you feel most frustrated, angry, agitated or hurt?

How?
- Do you fear the future?
- Do you feel isolated from your spouse because of illness?
- Are you struggling with anxiety or depression?
- Has your sex life changed or disappeared?
- Are you sleep-deprived, overwhelmed or fatigued?
- Has your social life been affected by chronic illness?
- Are you experiencing financial difficulties?
- Other:

8. What is the greatest change or most significant loss for *you* in your marriage?

9. Sit with God for a few minutes today and pray through the words of **1 Corinthians 13:4a**, *"Love is patient, love is kind."*

   Write these words on a Post-It note and place it where you will see them often. Ask God to show you one small act of kindness you can do for your spouse each day this week and write them here.

   Sunday:

   Monday:

   Tuesday:

   Wednesday:

Thursday:

Friday:

Saturday:

PRESSING ON:

10. How did your spouse respond to your acts of kindness?

    How did investing in small acts of kindness affect *you* this week?

There are no right or wrong answers; this is a place to wrestle with the impact of chronic illness on your marriage, an invitation to give yourself the time and space you need to work through some of the heartache, loss, grief, anger, frustration, weariness, anxiety, tension, and fear chronic illness has brought into your life and your marriage.

Take it slow. Allow God time and space to speak to your heart.

PRAYER:

Dear Heavenly Father, we so easily fail with this simple command of Yours in **Ephesians 4:32a**, "Be kind …" We come to You in our brokenness and humbly ask for You to work in and through our hearts and minds to show kindness to others, especially our spouses. Provide in us the patience, strength, and humility to put ourselves second in our marriage and to offer help, support, and love through kind and encouraging words. Amen.

Kindness Journal

Kindness Journal

[Love] does not envy, it does not boast ...
1 Corinthians 13:4b

Growth 2

"She held his hand like she never wanted to let him go." Those words replayed over and over in my mind as I cut the grass on a cool, overcast Tuesday afternoon. They were unusual words from my husband, and they caused me to pause and pray.

"Lord, is that what my husband wants — to know that he is so deeply loved that I never want to let him go?" The question simmered at the back of my mind for a couple of weeks. Then one afternoon I met a friend at the park and she asked how I was doing, wanting more than a cursory response. When I hesitated and shrugged, she questioned further. It had been a long few days of physical pain and I'd become quiet. Communicating when the pain is bad is difficult and often leaves me feeling isolated. Thoughts spring to mind, but speaking them out loud requires more energy than I'm sometimes willing to invest.

Ouch...

Those three small words, "willing to invest," sliced right through the quietness and into my soul. It had never occurred to me that selfishness had crept in when the pain was bad, and the realization that I'd allowed it to slink around for so long pained my heart. How often over the past dozen years had I expected my husband to know what I was feeling, to understand my sense of isolation, to ascertain my fear about what was happening to us?

Too often.

I expected my husband to read my mind, but he can't. Only God can, and even He doesn't want a one-sided relationship with me.

God longs to spend time with us, longs for us to hunger and thirst for His Word, longs for us to come to Him in prayer, to sit at His feet and rest in His presence. And if all that is true of God, how can it be any less true of my husband, who was created in His image?

My lack of words wasn't just isolating me, it was isolating my husband too, and suddenly his words began to make sense. We all long for relationship — deep, personal, intimate, honest relationship with God and with each other. We long to walk side by side through life, loving one another so deeply from the heart that we never want to let go.

STEPPING IN:

1. How does chronic illness affect the way you communicate with your spouse?

2. What is the most difficult thing to talk about with your spouse?

3. What is one activity you enjoy doing together? (For example, cooking together, taking a walk, praying together, going out to dinner, watching a movie or a favorite TV show, going to church.)

4. List one activity you would like to invite your spouse to do with you this week.

5. Think about a fun, creative way to invite your spouse. (For example, send a text; leave a Post-It note on her steering wheel; tuck a card into his briefcase, or lunch sack, etc.) Chances are it's been a while since you or your spouse invited each other on a date.

6. How did you feel initiating the date? Were you excited, anxious, fearful, frustrated, overwhelmed? It can feel quite vulnerable to step out in this way if chronic illness has caused some roadblocks in your marriage.

How did your spouse respond to your invitation?

How was your date?

If it didn't go as planned or if it didn't happen at all, that really is OK. It's a place to begin. Living with chronic illness means shifting perspective and learning to live together differently, to work together differently, to love one another differently.

And each time we try, we take a step toward our new "normal." That is love in action.

GOING DEEPER:

7. Read **Matthew 17:20b-21** and fill in the blanks:

    I tell you the _____, if you have _____ as _____ as a mustard seed, you can say to this _____, "_____ from here to there" and it _____ move. _____ will be _____ for you.

8. Let's start with a few words about mustard seeds.

    Mustard seeds are tiny – about 1-2mm in size. They germinate in approximately eight to ten days and reach a mature height of about 25 feet. Mustard plants grow wild throughout much of the Middle East and Africa, and can survive on less than eight inches of rain per year. Goats, camels and other desert grazers are drawn to the plant's moisture-rich leaves, and its tender young shoots have been used as natural teeth cleaners for hundreds of years.

So what does faith as small as a mustard seed have to do with chronic illness in marriage?

Often in a life with chronic illness, our fears and insecurities begin to weigh us down, making our lives feel small and unworthy ... like a mustard seed.

But that's exactly where Jesus steps in. He holds out His hand and says, "See? Faith no larger than *this* tiny seed is all you need. Why? Because your faith isn't based on this little seed, it's based on *Me*, the Author of life and the capstone of faith."

What size does your faith feel today?

- mustard seed
- pomegranate
- beach ball
- compact car
- motor home
- weeping willow
- spring-fed lake
- Dead Sea
- galaxy
- other

9. **Questions 4-6** were about a date with your spouse. Sometimes we need the opposite. Sometimes we need a little space and time for our emotions to settle, our hearts to calm, and our expectations to shift. That's what **Questions 7 and 8** were about. What's important here is not what you did or didn't do, or how your spouse responded (or didn't), it's about what God can do.

I TAKE YOU IN SICKNESS & IN HEALTH | 23

Faith as small as a mustard seed is all that we need to strengthen and encourage us for the journey ahead.

Based on this perspective shift, how would you describe your "date" with your spouse now, from the activity you chose to the invitation to how it all turned out (or maybe didn't)?

PRESSING ON:

10. Do you know your spouse's love language — the way he/she feels most loved and appreciated? Do you know yours? If not, consider taking the test together online at **5lovelanguages.com**. The Five Love Languages are:

    o words of affirmation
    o physical touch
    o receiving gifts
    o quality time
    o acts of service

    My love language is:

    My spouse's love language is:

PRAYER:

Dear Lord, show us Your way today. Allow in us the humility and patience needed to be vulnerable with our spouses, especially when it is the last thing we want to do. Help break down within us the pride that all too often gets in the way of speaking the truth in love, and learning to be more like You. Help us to openly share our hearts to each other just a little bit more each day and through this allow us to grow in our relationships with You and the ones to whom we said "I do." Amen.

Growth Journal

Growth Journal

[Love] is not proud.
1 Corinthians 13:4c

Willingness 3

My husband and I have faced things in this life we could never have imagined before experiencing them: the sudden death of my 32-year old brother, three job losses and relocations in six years, a serious car accident resulting in permanent injury, four of our five kids with significant, life-altering chronic illness, and the devastation of addiction, self-harm and unsuccessful suicide as three of our five longed to escape from chronic illness.

Marriage can be hard. And painful and lonely. *And dark*. There were times we stopped dreaming, times we were unable to communicate, times we survived as a couple *only* because we were each committed to our marriage. We didn't feel love, and sometimes, we didn't even like each other.

But we were committed. And sometimes that's enough. Sometimes commitment is the glue that gets you through.

When things were darkest, my husband and I continued to push through. We tried to communicate, tried to find each other again. And what we discovered is that we had to learn to *give each other grace*. We were under an enormous amount of pressure with four sick kids in their teens and early twenties, and honestly, we were all just trying to survive. Maybe it was OK that we were struggling. Maybe it was enough that we were committed. Maybe we needed to celebrate that we had survived *together* for more than twenty years through some incredibly trying circumstances. Maybe it was enough that we wanted more for our marriage and that we were committed to trying.

STEPPING IN:

1. Read **1 Kings 8:56a** and fill in the blanks:

   _____ be to the _____, who has given _____ to his _____ ...

2. Read **1 Kings 8:57a** and fill in the blanks:

   May the Lord _____ _____ be _____ us ...

3. Read **1 Kings 8:57b** and fill in the blanks:

   May he _____ leave us _____ forsake _____.

4. Read **1 Kings 8:58** and fill in the blanks:

   May he _____ our _____ to _____, to walk in _____ his _____ ...

5. Read **1 Kings 8:59** and fill in the blanks:

   And may these _____ of _____, which I have _____ before the _____, be _____ to the Lord our God _____ and _____, that he may _____ the _____ of his _____ and the

_____ of   his   _____   Israel   according   to

_____ day's _____ ...

6. Read **I Kings 8:60** and fill in the blanks:

   so   that   _____   the   peoples   of   the   _____   may

   _____ that the _____ is _____ and that

   there is no _____.

GOING DEEPER:

7. **1 Kings 8:56-60** is Solomon's prayer for the people with five specific requests:
   - God's presence
   - God's will in everything
   - each day's needs
   - the desire and ability to obey God's decrees and commands
   - the spread of God's kingdom on earth

   These five requests can become the cry of our hearts for our marriages and for our spouses. Today, pray each of these five requests for your husband or your wife.

   In the **Journal Pages** at the end of the chapter, write the specific points of your prayer and include the date. Commit to praying through these points for the next seven days and include where, when, and how you witness God at work.

   Praying for our marriages and our spouses is one of the most important, life-changing things we can do.

8. The deepest desire of our souls is for the *felt* nearness of God. Nothing is so needed and so sweet as the presence of God in our lives and in our marriages. God's grace is inexhaustible, and His mercy is unchanging.

    Where or how do *you* feel or experience God's presence in your life and in your marriage today?

9. Spend a few minutes today writing a prayer for your husband or wife in the **Journal Pages** at the end of this chapter. If you don't know where to begin, start by writing your spouse's name and listing just one thing you love, appreciate or respect about him or her.

    It can be as simple as, "I'm thankful my husband throws his dirty socks in the hamper," or "I'm thankful my wife always replaces the empty roll of toilet paper."

It can be a physical attribute, "I love my wife's deep brown eyes," or a skill, "I appreciate that my husband can fix our kitchen sink."

It can be for something you do together, "I'm grateful to attend church each week with my husband," or "I love that my wife makes our bed every day."

==Thinking about what we love, enjoy or appreciate about our spouse can begin to turn the tide.== As you move through the week and notice other things you're grateful for, add them to your prayer.

PRESSING ON:

10. Read **1 Corinthians 13:4** and fill in the blanks:

    _____ is _____, _____ is _____. It does _____ envy, it does _____ boast, it is _____ proud.

This is a wholly different kind of love than we see in the world around us. This is God's love poured out – selflessly, sacrificially, abundantly, expecting nothing in return.

Easy words to say. Hard words to live out. Especially when our marriages are strained physically, mentally, emotionally and/or spiritually by the ongoing grief and loss of chronic illness.

1 Corinthians 4:13 asks us to step beyond our cultural expectations and definitions of love, and beyond what we feel. It asks us to consider God's love poured out into His people for His sake.

For His sake. Those three words are key – ten letters that spin our understanding of love upside down and inside out. Because marriage is about so much more than us and our love. Marriage is all about *God* and *His love*, a gift none of us deserve, lavishly given, welling up and spilling over, poured out.

God's love asks us to be patient — "long-tempered," according to the original Greek, slow to anger. It asks us to endure personal wrongs, to bear with each other's imperfections, to give one another time to change and room to make mistakes.

Kindness is patience in action and is derived from the Greek word meaning "useful." A kind person is helpful, seeking out another's needs, looking for opportunities to meet those needs without repayment. Kindness is tender and calm, gentle and forgiving, quietly helping in practical ways.

In contrast, boasting seeks to puff us up, to make others jealous of what we have, of who we are, of what we're able to do. Envy breeds dissatisfaction and discontent, wanting what others have — bigger, better, faster, leaner, more.

God's love expects nothing in return.

Those are difficult words if your marriage is in crisis. But they are not impossible. This week, sit with those words. Ponder them. Pray through them. Speak them gently to yourself.

What do you hear God speaking to you through these words? If you need more space, there are **Journal Pages** at the end of this chapter for you to use.

PRAYER:

Dear Father in Heaven, help us as we go into this day to come to You, knowing we can't "do" this day without you. Allow in us a willingness to let go of whatever is getting in the way and preventing us from allowing You in. Change our hearts that can all too often become hardened toward our spouses and instead teach us to give grace to each other as You so freely give grace to us. Amen.

Willingness Journal

Willingness Journal

[Love] is not self-seeking ...
1 Corinthians 13:5b

Forgiveness 4

Forgiveness has been a difficult journey for my husband and I. We lost sight of each other somewhere along the way, not intentionally, but gradually. Tony grew increasingly immersed in work, as I was drowning in medical details — dozens of monthly appointments with dozens of specialists, coordinating medications and treatments, managing prolonged hospital stays, fighting for insurance coverage — and somehow in the midst of it all, homeschooling all five of our kids through high school.

The kids and I lived a life my husband knew little about. He didn't really understand their medical conditions, and was rarely able to attend their appointments. The harder life grew at home, the more Tony invested in his job, and the more distant I grew. Simultaneously, our kids, longing for a relationship with their dad, grew increasingly outspoken about his absence, bitterness creeping in and preparing to stay.

With our marriage at the breaking point and our family life wildly out of control, Tony made the difficult decision to retire early, come home and rescue us.

Six months later, he looked at me in bewilderment and said, "I had no idea. I knew our kids were sick, that you're sick, but I honestly had no idea what you were all going through. *I lived here and I had no idea.*"

We both had to learn to forgive. I had to accept that I, too, was responsible for where we'd wound up. I had stopped talking, stopped trying to explain, stopped asking for help. I had learned to figure things out, push through and do what needed to be done, but in the process, I had cut my husband out of the equation. The more self-sufficient I grew, the less my husband felt needed, and the less needed he felt, the more time and energy he poured into work. We were locked in a vicious cycle and the longer it continued, the further we drifted apart.

We both needed to learn to forgive before we could heal.

STEPPING IN:

1. Read **1 Corinthians 13:5b-c** and fill in the blanks:

   … it is not _____-_____, it is not _____

   _____ …

2. What do those words mean to you?

3. If love is not self-seeking and does not insist on its own way, *then love is the cure for selfishness.*

   Let those words sink in for a minute.

   Love is the cure for selfishness.

   What might happen today if you looked for opportunities to tenderly, gently, selflessly bless your husband or wife, expecting nothing in return?

4. What might happen if you chose to overlook your spouse's imperfections?

5. What might happen if you graciously recognized that each of you is going to make mistakes as you travel through life with chronic illness?

What if you each offered the other the time and space you each need to grieve?

6. Read **Psalm 103:11-12** and fill in the blanks:

   For as _____ as the _____ are above the _____, so _____ is his _____ for those who _____ him; as far as the _____ is from the _____, so far has _____ removed _____ transgressions from us.

   How do you describe a Renaissance painting to someone who is blind? How do you describe Handel's Hallelujah Chorus to someone who is deaf? How do you describe what it's like to run through fields or skip down the block to someone who has never been able to walk? How do you describe the infinite mercy, love and grace of God to finite human hearts?

GOING DEEPER:

7. Read **Psalm 103:8** and fill in the blanks:

   The Lord is _____ and _____, _____ to _____, _____ in _____.

What four things does this verse say about God's character?

-
-
-
-

8. **Psalm 103:8d** in the:

    o New Living Translation says, "filled with unfailing love."

    o English Standard Version says, "abounding in steadfast love."

    o New American Standard Bible says, "abounding in loving-kindness."

    o King James Bible says, "plenteous in mercy."

    o Christian Standard Version says, "his love never fails."

    o Good News Translation says," full of constant love."

    o Holman Christian Standard Bible says, "rich in faithful love."

    o Internal Standard Version says, "abundantly rich in gracious love."

Which of these translations speaks to your heart?

How do *you* most long to be loved?

9. Now look at this list of translations again and imagine choosing one to speak over your husband or your wife.

   Which one do you think your spouse most needs to hear *today*? Why?

   Write those words here.

PRESSING ON:

10. Forgiveness is the deepest form of love. It is also the most difficult, because forgiveness requires something valuable, extravagant, and vulnerable from us.

    Forgiveness requires sacrifice, choosing to see our spouse instead of their offense. Probably the most powerful example of forgiveness in Scripture is **Luke 23:34**.

    > *Father, forgive them, for they do not know what they are doing.*

    Jesus, from the cross, as He was dying, asked God to forgive those who were putting Him to death.

    Let that sink in for a moment.

    Jesus prayed *for* His enemies, *for* those who were torturing Him, and *for* all those who had wrongly accused Him of sins *He did not commit as* He was dying.

    Why? Because He loved them. *Because He loves* us.

    To forgive costs us something valuable and extravagant. To forgive is to willingly pardon, excuse, exonerate or absolve, to cancel a debt, to release our anger or resentment. To forgive, we must break the alabaster jar, place our last cent in the offering plate, wash our beloved's feet with our tears. To forgive is to lower our guard and meet God in this broken place of chronic illness, in the hardships and trials of our marriage, and to release the pain, placing it in God's hands, allowing Him to hold the burden we cannot, to fill us with His abounding, steadfast, never-failing, rich, gracious, abundant, and faithful love.

    Turn to the **Journal Pages** at the end of this chapter and write out your prayer to God. Place what you can no longer carry in His hands. Let it go. Lay it down. Release the pain. Release the anger. Release the expectations. And just come. Open your hands. Let go of the fear, the guilt, the shame.

    Often, we feel responsible for our illnesses, or bitterness toward our spouse's, and those feelings require forgiveness in order for us to heal and move forward together. Forgiveness begins with love. And tender love fully realized ripens into greater forgiveness.

Speak the words of **Ephesians 2:10** (below) over you and your spouse this week to remind you of who you each are, who you were created to be, and what you are both called to do.

"For we are God's workmanship, created in Christ Jesus to do good works, which God prepared in advance for us to do."

PRAYER:

Lord, I need You. I've held on too long to my own pain and hurt, and struggled to find forgiveness, especially when it's hard. Help me to see through Your eyes and not my own, so that I may understand, in some small way, the pain and struggles of others. Open my heart and mind to compassion for others so I can be a help and an example, in some small way, of Your unfailing love. Restore the love between me and my spouse as only You can. Amen.

Forgiveness Journal

Forgiveness Journal

Love is not easily angered, it keeps no record of wrongs.
1 Corinthians 13:5c

Time 5

Time together has become a non-negotiable in our lives. With our marriage strained to the breaking point, Tony and I finally carved out weekly "date nights" with each other and wrote them on the calendar. In ink. Many of those evenings were painful and uncomfortable. Some nights we barely talked. Some nights we argued. Some nights we left the restaurant feeling frustrated and angry. Many nights I cried. A few times it took everything in me to stay in that booth all the way through dinner.

But we persevered. And as we did, something happened.

We began to talk. *Really talk*. About the good stuff, the hard stuff, the things that hurt. We still stumbled through anger and frustration. We still sometimes found ourselves guarded and uncomfortable, but we also began to laugh. We began to remember the good times. We sometimes dared to dream. Some nights we left the restaurant smiling.

Some nights, the tears were good.

Months into the journey, we added occasional overnights into our routine, something we each look forward to. We aren't gone long — about 24 hours — but its enough time for us to reconnect as a couple. We don't do anything fancy. Sometimes, we don't even leave the hotel room. For it's a respite – uninterrupted, unhurried, and unscheduled time for just the two of us.

Because time, we're learning, is not a luxury. It's a necessity, and it's vital to a strong and healthy marriage.

STEPPING IN:

1. Read **Psalm 90:12** and fill in the blanks:

    _____ _____ to _____ our _____ aright, that we may _____ a _____ of _____.

    Psalm 90 is a psalm of prayer and the only psalm attributed to Moses.

    Ephesians 5:15 tells us to "Be very careful, then, how you live …"

    Time holds intrinsic value. **Psalm 90** reminds us to examine our days, to be grateful for the gift of time, to recognize both its earthly *and* eternal value.

    - If you want to understand the value of a year, ask a parent who has lost a child.
    - If you want to understand the value of a month, ask the mother of a premature infant.
    - If you want to understand the value of a week, ask a student who just completed final exams.
    - If you want understand the value of a day, ask a day laborer with a family to feed.
    - If you want to understand the value of an hour, ask the surgeon who just completed a complicated transplant.
    - If you want to understand the value of a minute, ask the person who just missed a train, a plane or a bus.
    - If you want to understand the value of a second, ask those who have lost a loved one in a single faulty heartbeat.
    - If you want to understand the value of a millisecond, ask an Olympic silver medalist.

Time not only carries inherent, intrinsic, earthly and eternal value, it is also a uniquely fixed resource. We can't save it, sell it or stockpile it. Every minute of every day, regardless of how we use it, is a fixed rate of 60 seconds.

2. Read **Ephesians 5:15-16a** and fill in the blanks:

   Be very _____, then, how you _____ — not as unwise but as _____, making the _____ of _____ opportunity..."

3. "[M]aking the most of every opportunity ..." That's a tall order. Today, in the **Journal Pages** at the end of this chapter, spend some time exploring what your marriage might look like *if*, instead of holding onto the pain, anger, frustration, guilt, shame, expectations, bitterness, or feelings of responsibility for the illness, you chose to make the *most of every opportunity*.

   How would that change the way you live today?

4. **In Psalm 39**, David explores the meaning of time, asking God to "Show me, O Lord ... the number of my days ..."

   Ecclesiastes 11:8 tells us how to live into the gift of those days: "However many years a man may live, let him enjoy them all."

   "...let him enjoy them all." Good words, but how do we do that?

   - By savoring each moment
   - Being fully present
   - Loving God and loving others

- Being grateful for what we have, what we can do, and each hour we've been given

5. Read **Psalm 39:5** and fill in the blanks:

   _____ have made my _____ a mere _____; the span of my _____ is as _____ before you. Each _____ life is _____ a _____.

   Read **Psalm 39:11b** and fill in the blanks:

   … _____ _____ is _____ a _____.

   A handbreadth is the width of the palm below the four fingers (not including the thumb) – approximately 2½ to 4 inches — a very small measure when associated with the span of a human life. Yet in light of eternity, our lives *are* but a handbreadth.

   And because of sin, they are also filled with loss. Loss and the accompanying journey through grief have a powerful way of stripping away the noise, the peripheral, the unimportant, and focusing us instead on God.

6. Read **Psalm 40:17b** and fill in the blanks:

   You are my _____ and my _____; O my God, do _____ delay."

BUILDING A BUCKET LIST

Have you and your spouse ever built a bucket list?

Bucket lists are ways of charting our hopes and dreams, and the things we'd love to see and experience before we die.

You can write a bucket list for each season of the year, or for specific seasons of life.

Bucket list items don't have to be extreme or expensive. They can include things like going to a new restaurant or a concert in the park, learning to play chess or learning to write a memoir, watching the sunrise or lining the driveway with luminarias on Christmas or New Year's Eve.

Bucket lists are a wonderful opportunity for you and your spouse to begin to dream together again.

A BUCKET LIST IN FIVE STEPS

1. What matters most to you? What are your core values? What do you hold most dear?

2. What would you like to experience in this season of your life? In the next ten years?

3. Brainstorm ideas for your bucket list. Consider:
   - Places to see
   - Things to do
   - Skills to learn

- Family and friends to visit
- Projects to start (or finish)
- Causes to support
- Regrets to resolve
- People to forgive
- Sports, hobbies or activities to try
- Books to read
- Topics to learn about
- Healthy new goals or habits
- Random acts of kindness you can participate in together

4. Now create a timeline. What would you like to experience first, in the next year, in the next five years?

5. Prioritize your list based on your time and energy, and on the things you and your spouse hold most valuable.

QUESTIONS, IDEAS AND CONVERSATION STARTERS

To get you started, we've developed a list of 101 questions and conversations starters. Choose one or two over the next several weeks as you rekindle your dreams *together*.

1. When was the last time you tried something new? What did you do?
2. What's the best advice you've ever been given?
3. What lesson did you learn the hard way?
4. What would you do today if you knew you wouldn't be judged?
5. If you could wake up tomorrow with a new skill, what would it be?
6. Where would you most like to go?
7. Who would you most like to visit?
8. What was your favorite childhood book or movie?
9. What kind of food would you like to try?
10. What show or performance would you like to see?

11. What hobby would you love to learn?
12. What random act of kindness would it be fun to do together?
13. Is there someone you need to forgive?
14. What is your dream vacation?
15. Who has had a powerful impact on your life? Have you ever told them?
16. What three things make your life easier?
17. What makes you laugh?
18. What would give you the greatest confidence boost?
19. If you could start a business with no strings attached, what would it be?
20. What were you passionate about as a child that you'd love to try again?
21. What would you like more of in your life?
22. What are the five things you're most thankful for?
23. What is the most adventurous thing you've ever done?
24. What do you like most about your appearance?
25. Over the last five yours, how have you've changed?
26. If you could take a year long sabbatical what would you do? Where would you go?
27. What movie scene would you like to experience in real life?
28. What are you holding onto that you need to let go?
29. What makes you smile?
30. If you had the opportunity to address to an audience, what would you say?
31. What is important enough to go to war over?
32. What is something you do differently than most people?
33. What are you most grateful for?
34. What is the one thing you'd most like to change in the world?
35. What inspires you?
36. Describe your life in six words.
37. What is the most defining moment of your life?
38. What is your most beloved childhood memory?
39. What gives your life meaning?
40. What is your life's purpose?
41. What is the most memorable gift you have received?
42. Describe the last three months of your life in three words.
43. Describe what freedom means to you.
44. What is your greatest challenge?
45. If you could live one day over again, which day would you choose?

46. If you could invite anyone to dinner, living or dead, who would you choose?
47. Why do you matter?
48. What makes you think of *home*?
49. What is your most prized possession?
50. What is your greatest accomplishment?
51. What makes a person beautiful?
52. Where do you find peace?
53. When have you worked hard and loved every minute of it?
54. Who do you trust and why?
55. If you had to give up every physical possession except what could fit in a single backpack, what would you keep?
56. When does silence speak louder than words?
57. What is your greatest skill?
58. What do you have trouble seeing clearly in your mind?
59. What are you looking forward to?
60. Who is the strongest person you know?
61. What makes today worth living?
62. What is your favorite song and why?
63. What makes you angry?
64. What is the most valuable lesson you learned from your parents?
65. What does love feel like?
66. What is the best part of growing older?
67. What is worth waiting for?
68. Where would you most like to live? Why?
69. What is your greatest strength?
70. What is your greatest weakness?
71. What made you smile this week?
72. What motivates you to do your best?
73. What is the most spontaneous thing you've ever done?
74. What life lessons did you have to experience before you understood them?
75. What is your saddest memory?
76. What is the best decision you've ever made?
77. What makes love last?
78. What is your greatest distraction?
79. What do you think about when you like awake in bed?
80. What responsibility would delegate if you could?

81. Who do you secretly envy and why?
82. What is your favorite sound?
83. What makes you cry?
84. Describe your childhood in one word.
85. What is your spouse's most attractive quality?
86. What is the last thing that surprised you?
87. What is your biggest pet peeve?
88. What is the best compliment you have received?
89. When was your first impression of someone completely wrong?
90. What is the number one quality of a good leader?
91. Where is your favorite place on earth?
92. In what ways are you your own worst enemy?
93. What is your favorite quote?
94. What do you know well enough to teach others?
95. What stresses you out?
96. What do you want more of in life?
97. What do you want less of in life?
98. What is your favorite smell?
99. What is your favorite holiday?
100. What simple fact do you wish more people understood?
101. Describe your future in three words.

BUCKET LIST IDEAS

Still stuck? Start small by choosing from the list below. Sometimes all it takes is the first step to spark a new dream.

1. Go for a walk.
2. Look up at the night sky.
3. Hold hands in the car.
4. Curl up on the couch and talk.
5. Have a picnic in the backyard or at a local park.
6. Volunteer together for a worthwhile cause.
7. Cook dinner together.
8. Mail each other a handwritten letter.

9. Watch the sunrise or sunset together.
10. Read a book out loud to each other.
11. Kiss in the rain.
12. Memorize a favorite passage of the Bible.
13. Look for funny moments. Laugh more. Let your joy become contagious.
14. Create a Reverse Bucket List – an exercise in gratefulness. Write a list of all the things you've done, places you've gone, adventures you've experienced, people you've visited, etc.
15. Attend a book reading in support of a local author.
16. Visit a local museum.
17. Plant a flower or a tree.
18. Dye Easter eggs.
19. Splash in a puddle.
20. Make homemade hot cocoa.
21. Decorate sugar cookies.
22. Complete a "Random Act of Kindness" together.
23. Carve a pumpkin.
24. Share a milkshake.
25. Have a bubblegum blowing contest.
26. Fly a kite.
27. Visit a hometown attraction.
28. Play a board game.
29. Solve a jigsaw puzzle.
30. Renew your wedding vows.
31. Recreate your first date.
32. Slow dance at home.
33. Start a journal of love letters to each other.
34. Attend a couple's retreat.
35. Begin a couple's devotional.
36. Enjoy a concert in the park.
37. Build a house of cards.
38. Volunteer at a soup kitchen, homeless shelter, humane society, or wildlife refuge.
39. Build a birdhouse.
40. Take a class together.
41. Go to a farmers market.

42. Kiss under the mistletoe.
43. Do a Word Find.
44. Make a gingerbread house.
45. Go on a dessert date.

AN ETERNAL BUCKET LIST

Now that you're on your way, consider another kind of bucket list — one with eternity in mind.

Read **Matthew 25:35-36** and fill in the blanks.

For I was _____ and you gave me something to _____, I was _____ and you gave me something to _____, I was a _____ and you _____ _____ _____, I needed _____ and you _____ me, I was _____ and you _____ _____ _____, I was in _____ and you came to _____ me.

Here, we read about six specific things we are called to do:
- Feed the hungry
- Give drink to the thirsty
- Clothe the naked
- Shelter the homeless
- Visit the sick
- Visit those in prison

But there's more. Read **1 Peter 4:10** and fill in the blanks:

Each of you should _____ whatever _____ he has received

to _____ others, _____ _____ God's grace in

its _____ forms.

Begin thinking about your gifts, your skill sets, and what you love to do? Think big and small. Spend some time brainstorming. For example:

- yard work
- accounting
- house cleaning
- financial planning/debt management
- laundry
- plumbing
- painting
- electrical work
- cooking/baking
- auto repair
- errands
- carpentry
- volunteering
- correspondence/writing
- computer programming
- sewing, knitting, crocheting
- gardening
- crafts
- decorating
- photography
- salon services (hair cuts, beard trims, perms, etc.)
- music lessons
- home organization
- listening

Look back at **Matthew 25:35-36** and **1 Peter 4:10**.

Use these seven tenets to build your Eternal Bucket List. Have fun with this. Dream together. Pray together. Ask God to guide and inspire you. Here's a short list to help you begin.

ETERNAL BUCKET LIST IDEAS

A. **Feed the Hungry**
   - Make sandwiches for the homeless
   - Purchase groceries for someone who is struggling financially
   - Volunteer at a rescue mission or soup kitchen
   - Donate to a food pantry
   - Make a meal for someone who is ill, recovering from surgery, unable to drive, or homebound

B. **Give "A Cup of Cold Water" to the Thirsty**
   - Donate water bottles for the homeless
   - Donate baby formula to a pregnancy help center
   - Volunteer at a drink station during a charity race
   - Pay for the person in line behind you at a coffee shop

C. **Clothe the Naked**
   - Clean out your closet, attic, garage or basement and donate what you no longer need
   - Knit, crochet or sew baby blankets for a pregnancy help center
   - Donate scarves, hats, socks, jackets, mittens or boots to a homeless shelter

D. **Shelter the Homeless**
   - Volunteer on a local Habitat for Humanity worksite
   - Mentor a child through Big Brothers/Big Sisters or a similar organization
   - Sponsor a child through Compassion International, World Relief or a similar organization
   - Volunteer at or donate to a local rescue mission or homeless shelter

E. **Visit the Sick**
   - Volunteer at a hospital
   - Volunteer at a nursing home
   - Send a card to someone in the hospital, someone recovering from surgery, someone going through cancer treatment or someone who is homebound

F. **Visit Those in Prison**
   - Lead a Bible study at a jail or prison
   - Donate Bibles or spiritual resource s to a jail, prison or correction center
   - Mentor a troubled teen
   - Become a pen pal through Prison Fellowship, Evangel Prison Ministries, Christian PenPal Ministry, or a similar organization

G. **Use Your Gifts**
   - Make a meal
   - Alter a dress
   - Teach a skill you have
   - Be a mentor
   - Use the gifts God has given you to enrich the lives of others

Bucket lists can help us remember who we are and why we're here. They can draw us closer as a couple and deeper into God as we pour the love, compassion, mercy and grace He so freely lavishes on us into the hearts and lives of those around us.

In short, a bucket list can help us:

- dream together as a couple
- love God, our spouses and others well
- prioritize where and how we invest our time, energy, skills, and resources
- bring glory to God as we learn to live out his Word

GOING DEEPER:

7. Now let's go back to where it all began – to your wedding day. Pull out a photo from that day and walk through all the details you can remember.

   What month was it?

   Where did your ceremony take place?

Who was there?

How did you feel? Excited? Nervous?

Did anything funny happen?

Anything surprising?

Do you remember the colors you chose or the cake?

Do you remember your vows?

As you look back on that day and out across the weeks, months or years that have brought you to *this* day, what stands out to you?

Pause here in this place of remembering for as long as you need.

Sometimes we need to a little time and space to look back at where we've been in order to see more clearly where we're going.

8. As you look at your marriage through eternity's lens, what would you miss most if you unexpectedly lost your husband or wife today?

9. Read **James 4:14** and fill in the blanks:

   Why, you do not even _____ what will happen _____.

   What is your _____? You are a _____ that appears for

   a little _____ and then _____. Instead, you ought to

   say, "_____ it is the _____ _____, we

   will live to _____ _____ or _____."

PRESSING ON:

10. Today, write down the three *most* important things about your husband or wife, about your marriage, and about your lives together.

PRAYER:

Dear Heavenly Father, all too often I take for granted the time I have here on earth and lose sight of the gift that it is. Help me to look differently at the time you have granted me with, to make the most of this precious gift, which can end at any moment. Help me to value every moment, every minute and every second to do good in my marriage, especially when it is hard, and through this to glorify and honor you. Amen.

Time Journal

Time Journal

Love ... rejoices with the truth.
1 Corinthians 13:6

Intimacy 6

Intimacy – to be wholly known and wholly loved – is the deepest desire of the human heart. All of humanity was created for each other, members of *One* Body, *together* the bride of Christ.

Marriage is the sacred joining of two into *one*. A holy gift it took me years to grasp, not because it satisfies desire or for its role in procreation, though those are blessings too, but because intimacy fosters unity, harmony, and peace, drawing us into deeper relationship with one God and one another.

In our marriage, intimacy has been a doorway to trust and vulnerability, and a powerful connection on our darkest days when words were few. Intimacy has nurtured not only patience and forgiveness, but greater understanding and stronger communication.

That I love my husband *more* after 25 years of marriage than I did on the day we walked down the aisle, that I find him more attractive at 60 than on the day we married, and that we enjoy one another more in middle age than we did as newlyweds, still surprises and delights me.

But isn't that just like God? To draw us deeper into love as we learn to more wholly love and be loved?

Glimpses of eternity. One Body. *Together*. On holy ground.

STEPPING IN:

1. Read **Genesis 2:20** and fill in the blanks:

    So the _____ gave _____ to all the _____, the _____ of the _____ and all the _____ of the _____. But for _____ no _____ _____ was found.

    Let that sink in for a minute. *"But for Adam no suitable helper was found."* Adam was walking in the Garden with every single creature on earth. He knew them. He'd named them. Creatures of every size and shape and color. And yet for Adam, no suitable helper was found, for there was no one *like* him.

2. Read **Genesis 2:21-22** and fill in the blanks:

    So the Lord _____ the man to fall into a _____ _____; and while he was sleeping, he _____ one of the man's _____ and _____ up the place with _____. Then the Lord _____ _____ a _____ from the _____ he had _____ out of the _____, and he brought _____ to the _____.

    Again, think about this. God could have created woman as He had created every other living creature. He didn't need Adam's rib to form Eve, yet He chose to do something different.

3. Adam acknowledges that in **Genesis 2:23**:

   The man said, "_____ is now _____ of my _____ and _____ of my _____; she shall be called '_____' for she was taken out of man."

   This relationship between Adam and Eve, between man and woman, has been different from the start.

   Genesis 2:23a ESV says: "Then the man said, 'This *at last* is bone of my bones and flesh of my flesh" (Emphasis mine.)

   "This at last," Adam says. It's almost as if he had been waiting, holding his breath, somehow sensing that Eve was just around the next bend.

4. Let's roll back the clock today. Think back to the first time you met your husband or wife. What was the first thing you noticed?

   Do you remember what he or she was wearing?

   Do you remember where you were?

Were others with you?

Do you remember what you said?

Do you remember how you felt?

Fast-forward to your first date.

What were you wearing?

Where did you go?

What did you do?

Were others with you?

Did anything surprise you?

Did anything delight you?

What specifically did you notice about your husband or wife?

5. When did you know you were in love? Can you remember the exact moment or was it a slow, gentle development?

Did you tell your husband or wife right away or did it take some time to work up the courage?

6. Now let's look the **Song of Solomon**, some of the most beautifully intimate verses in the Bible.

   Read Song of Solomon 1:2 and fill in the blanks:

   Let him _____ me with the _____ of his _____ — for your _____ is more _____ than _____.

   Do you remember your first kiss?

   Do you remember where you were?

   Do you remember what time of year it was?

   Was it sweet or passionate or awkward?

   Did it make your knees go weak?

I TAKE YOU IN SICKNESS & IN HEALTH | 75

GOING DEEPER:

7. Read **Song of Solomon 1:15a** and fill in the blanks:

    How _____ you are, my _____! Oh, how _____!

    Read **Song of Solomon 1:16a** and fill in the blanks:

    How _____ you are, my _____! Oh, how _____!

    Did you call each other sweet nicknames or by terms of endearment when you were dating or early in your marriage? If so, what were they?

    Do you and your spouse have nicknames or terms of endearment for each other today?

8. Read **Song of Solomon 1:6** and fill in the blanks:

    Do not _____ at _____ because I am _____, because _____ _____ darkened by the sun.

Solomon's beloved was self-conscious about her appearance under his gaze – a struggle as old as time.

9. Read **Song of Solomon 2:3** and fill in the blanks:

   Like an _____ tree _____ the _____ of

   the _____ is my _____ among the _____

   _____. I _____ to sit in his _____, and

   his _____ is _____ to my _____.

   She praises Solomon, recognizing him as the finest of all the young men "of the forest." She is not only proud *of* him, she is proud to be *with* him, proud to be seen in his presence.

   Did you feel that way once? Proud of your husband or wife? Proud to be with him or her? Proud to be seen in his or her presence? These might be difficult questions to answer or even to think through today, and that's OK. Take it slow. Sometimes we have to remember in order to heal.

PRESSING ON:

10. In **Chapter 5, Question 7**, you pulled out a photograph from your wedding to remind you of the day it all began.

    Read **Song of Solomon 3:11** and fill in the blanks:

    Come out, you _____ of Zion, and _____ at King

    Solomon _____ the _____, the crown with which his

    _____ crowned _____ on the _____ of his

    _____, the _____ his _____ rejoiced.

"... the day his heart rejoiced." Did your heart rejoice on your wedding day?

On your wedding night?

Does it still rejoice today?

Take some time over the next few days to write your husband or wife a letter. Include some of the details from when you first met, from your first date, your first kiss, your nicknames for each other, from your wedding day, from your wedding night. Close with something specific about your spouse that still surprises or delights you. Then leave it someplace where it will surprise or delight your spouse — taped to the bathroom mirror, under her favorite mug, on his car seat, in her briefcase, on his pillow, in her gym bag.

PRAYER:

Lord, you have given us the beautiful gift of intimacy and you remind us in Matthew 19:5b, "and the two will become one flesh." All too often we view intimacy as something it is not and we miss out on the importance it has in our marriage relationship. Help us, Father, to understand and appreciate how special this time together can be, how it can break down barriers and heal hurts and create a special bond between us. Help us not to miss out on the true meaning of intimacy as You meant it to be in our marriages — beautiful, loving and kind. Amen.

Intimacy Journal

Intimacy Journal

*Love always protects, always trusts,
always hopes, always perseveres.*
1 Corinthians 13:7

Differences 7

Differences are good. This is something I didn't understand when we got married. And it's something my husband and I are still learning after 26 years of marriage. Life is hard and beautiful and tragic and amazing. And we are all human.

We each bring different gifts and perspectives to our marriage, and those differences are *GOOD*. They can be frustrating and exasperating, but they can also be brilliant. My husband sees the big picture from 20,000 feet, though sometimes misses important details. I notice the details, but sometimes forget there's life beyond my own myopic line of sight.

It's not that one of us is right and one of us is wrong. It's that we need *both*. We're better together. Yes, we're going to scrape up against each other sometimes, but those are often the times that iron sharpens iron, resulting in a better decision together than either one of us could make apart.

How we solve conflict, how we eat or dream or plan our days, how we handle money or time or pain or illness, how we celebrate the holidays or clean the house, how we care for family or spend our free time *will be different*. Yet those moments when we chafe against each other's rough edges and weary spirits, is actually an opportunity, a chance to offer patience and forgiveness, to extend kindness and understanding, to step off the mountain of self and willingly stand *together* in the trenches.

STEPPING IN:

1. Read **Proverbs 27:17** and fill in the blanks:

   As iron _____ iron, so one _____ sharpens _____.

   We often think of this verse in terms of differences in styles, skills, characteristics or abilities. But what about in terms of chronic illness?

   What has been the biggest change in how you and your spouse relate *because of chronic illness*?

2. Read **Romans 15:5-6** and fill in the blanks:

   May the God who _____ _____ and _____ give you a spirit of _____ among yourselves as you _____ Christ Jesus, so that with _____ _____ and mouth you may _____ the God and Father of our Lord _____ _____.

   At first glance, **Proverbs 27:17** and **Romans 15:5-6** seem contradictory. How can we simultaneously *need each other's differences* and also pray for "a spirit of unity"?

   Yet what if the question isn't either/or, but both/and? What if we need our spouse's *differences* to sharpen and hone our understanding, to refine and clarify our vision so that *together*, with *unity of heart*, we can glorify God?

3. Differences in a marriage can be challenging without chronic illness, but when illness becomes a prominent member of the marriage, differences can feel like personal attacks.

   This week, we're going to examine what has changed in your marriage relationship since chronic illness came to stay.

   On a scale of 1 to 10 with 1 being in crisis and 10 being content, circle where you feel your marriage is right now.

   1   2   3   4   5   6   7   8   9   10

4. Let's take a look at 12 specific characteristics of strong relationships. Did you notice that's one characteristic for each month of the year? These verses, built on the cornerstone of Jesus Christ, can help us build vibrant, thriving marriage relationships in the midst of chronic illness.

   Read **Ephesians 3:14-21** and fill in the blanks:

   For this _____ I kneel before the _____, from whom his whole family in heaven and on earth derives its name. I _____ that out of the _____ _____ he may _____ you with _____ through his _____ in your inner being, so that _____ may _____ in your _____ through _____. And I _____ that you, being _____ and _____ in _____, may have _____, _____ with _____ the _____, to grasp how _____ and _____ and _____ and _____ is the _____ of

_____, and to know _____ love that _____ knowledge — that you may be _____ to the _____ of all the _____ of _____. Now to _____ who is _____ to do _____ than all we _____ or _____, according to _____ power that is _____ _____ within us, to him be the _____ in the church and in Christ Jesus throughout _____ generations, for ever and ever! Amen.

Pray these words for your husband or wife today. Pray them for yourself. God's love is *complete*, encompassing more than we can imagine, stretching beyond our finite grasp of time, higher than our greatest joy, and deeper than our most crushing pain.

He is able to do immeasurably more than all we ask or imagine ...

Sit with those words today. If we prayed just those 13 words every day for one month, what do you think might change?

5. Read **Proverbs 3:5-6** and fill in the blanks:

_____ in the _____ with _____ your

_____ and _____ _____ on your

_____ understanding; in _____ your

_____ acknowledge _____, and _____

will make _____ paths _____.

These verses speak to the expectations we too often place not only on ourselves, but also on our spouse. We can think of expectations a little like we think of dynamite. We see it and recognize it, we have a basic understanding of its power, but without a clear expectation for its use, we can be caught completely off-guard.

The beautiful part of these verses draws us to lean away from our own understanding and into God's. To lean means to rest our full weight against, to rely on, depend on, trust in.

Who are we called to place our trust in? The Lord, who is able – so much more than able. Always and forever able.

Think about and note the expectations you have of yourself and also of your spouse. Did those change because of chronic illness? Use the **Journal Pages** at the end of this chapter to explore this question.

6. Read **Colossians 3:12-14** and fill in the blanks:

Therefore, as God's _____ people, _____ and _____ loved, _____ yourselves with _____, _____, _____, _____ and _____. Bear with each other and _____ whatever _____ you may have _____ one another. _____ as the Lord _____ you. And over all these virtues _____ _____, which binds them all together in _____ _____.

Read those words slowly. Read them aloud. Savor each one. Let them nourish your soul. For you are chosen. You are holy. And you are dearly loved.

Do you believe that?

Because that's where it all begins. Before we can love one another, we must first know how radically, passionately, and perfectly we are loved by God.

GOING DEEPER:

7. Look at the list of expectations you wrote in the **Journal Pages** for **Question 5**. Begin with the expectations you place on yourself. In light of these verses, how do those expectations change?

8. How do your expectations of your spouse change in light of **Colossians 3:12-14**?

We all long to be chosen – to be treated with kindness, compassion, humility, gentleness and patience, to be *borne with*, and forgiven.

In short, we all *long to be loved*, deeply from the heart.

Yet we are also human, and while our spirits are willing, our flesh is weak. We are subject to distraction of all kinds: hunger, thirst, selfishness, exhaustion, frustration, anger, bitterness, worry, jealousy, pride, pain, fear, laziness, greed, and gossip.

The answer is *to watch for and pray* (**Matthew 26:41a**) – to watch for temptation and to pray for God's strength in our weakness.

9. Read **Galatians 6:10a** and fill in the blanks:

Therefore, as we _____ _____, let us

_____ _____ to _____ people …

This verse might make you angry. It might overwhelm you. It might make you question this study. It might make you question me. And that's OK. After all, in our own strength, we *can't* do this. In our own strength, we get stuck in the pain, stuck in the sorrow, stuck in the suffering, and stuck in our expectations.

But in the long, dark winter of the soul, it is the tender new shoot that pushes up through winter-hardened soil in search of sunlight.

Today, choose one small way to encourage your spouse. For example:
- Make her coffee
- Wipe down the kitchen counter
- Offer a hug
- Clean a toilet
- Make the bed
- Bake his favorite dessert
- Invite her to dance in the kitchen or for a walk around the block
- Feed the dog
- Massage his shoulders
- Offer a sincere compliment

PRESSING ON:

10. Today, I want to ask you a question that might take a little bit of time to answer. Turn to the **Journal Pages** at the end of this chapter and draw a line down the middle of a page. On the left side list your attributes, all those qualities in you that are vibrant and good. Across the page from those qualities, list their opposites – how each attribute can also be a weakness.

    For example: One of my son's greatest strengths is perseverance, but when perseverance hardens into stubbornness, it can be one of his greatest weaknesses.

    My daughter takes much of life in stride, a great attribute, but the flip side of that strength is laziness, a challenging weakness.

Set aside some time over the next few days to work on this assignment. You will find two different **Character Quality Journal Pages** at the end of this chapter – one for you and one for you to list what you see in your spouse. When you have each completed your lists, find time to talk about them together.

PRAYER:

Dear Father in Heaven, You have graciously blessed each of us with qualities both different and unique. Forgive us when those differences anger or annoy us, or become qualities we are critical of. Help us to understand that You use those differences for *good*, opportunities to understand and treat others with kindness, patience and compassion. Allow us to see how the "shortcomings" of others are actually "shortcomings" in us, opportunities for our growth. Let us see the beauty in all of this and how it can bring us into closer in relationship with You. Amen.

Differences Journal

Differences Journal

Differences Journal
Character Qualities - Self

Differences Journal
Character Qualities - Spouse

Do everything in love.
1 Corinthians 16:14

Presence 8

As I sat in the hospital cafeteria one afternoon with a friend, she offered her help in myriad ways — providing meals, watching my kids (girls, boys, overnight, just days, her house, my house), and more. While I truly appreciated her offers, I was overwhelmed by the thought of not only coordinating, but effectively communicating medication schedules and special diets for my kids. I understood her desire to help, to do something physical, tangible, and practical, yet all I could manage was, "I honestly don't know, but I'll think about it, *really*, and let you know." She paused and quietly replied, "You're a very hard woman to come alongside in a crisis."

My friend is right. She wasn't judging me or being harsh. She'd thoughtfully offered the help she knew I needed, but I was holding her at arm's length doing the only thing I know to do when things get hard — move forward one step at a time doing whatever needs to be done next.

Throughout the afternoon, my friend's words hovered at the edge of my thoughts, and slowly, bit by bit, revealed a surprising truth. When crisis hits, my perspective shifts and all that exists is the present moment. I am simply, completely, fully immersed in the moment. What a revelation! As I allowed that thought to sink in, I began to understand what an unexpectedly precious gift comes wrapped in crisis packaging. God was graciously offering me unhurried, distraction-free, intimately-focused time with the man I love most in this world, not in a way I would have chosen, but in a way I couldn't diminish.

Hour after hour, day after day as I sat beside my husband in the hospital, I was simply there. My mind wasn't processing extraneous details. I wasn't distracted by laundry or email or papers that needed to be graded. I wasn't answering the phone or cutting up vegetables.

I was simply there, aware of the gentle, rhythmic pumping of the IV, the muffled voices of the nursing staff outside the door, the steady ticking of the clock, my husband's breathing, the quiet rustle of his sheets. I was fully engaged in the moment.

And that's when it hit me. Isn't that how we're supposed to live, *fully engaged*? Not just in crisis, but in every moment of every day of our lives? So fully present that we don't miss a thing, not a single blessing? Why do we allow ourselves to become so distracted and scattered, so over-committed and busy and stressed that we take all we've been given for granted?

Why do we so often fail to understand what we've got till it's gone?

STEPPING IN:

1. Today, we're going to step back a few centuries and explore the ancient Prayer of Examen.

   More than prayer, *Examen* is a practice that draws us into the Presence of God. It is a retuning, a refocusing in order to reflect on the day and discover God's Presence in the midst of it.

   Examen brings us into a deeper awareness of God's Presence (*consciousness*), revealing to us where we need forgiveness (*conscience*). At its heart, Examen is simply sharing our day with Jesus and seeking His direction through prayer.

   Let's begin with the words of **Lamentations 3:19-26.**

   I remember my affliction and my wandering,
   the bitterness and the gall.
   I well remember them,
   and my soul is downcast within me.
   Yet this I call to mind
   and therefore I have hope:
   Because of the Lord's great love we are not consumed,
   for His compassions never fail.
   They are new every morning;
   great is your faithfulness.
   I say to myself, "The Lord is my portion;
   therefore I will wait for him."
   The Lord is good to those whose hope is in him,
   to the one who seeks him;
   it is good to wait quietly
   for the salvation of the Lord.

2. Read this passage several times. What do you notice about it?

3. How does the prophet Jeremiah begin in lines 1-4?

   What is his state of mind?

   What is he wrestling with?

4. Read **Lamentations 3:1a** and fill in the blanks:

   I am the _____ who has seen _____ ...

   Jeremiah goes on to say, "He has driven me away ... made me walk in darkness ... turned his hand against me ... made my skin and flesh grow old ... besieged me and surrounded me with bitterness and hardship ... made me dwell in darkness ... walled me in ... weighed me down ... he shuts out my prayer ... He has barred my way ... he dragged me away ... mangled me ... left me without help ... made me the target for his arrows ... pierced my heart ... filled me with bitter herbs and sated me with gall ... broken my teeth ... trampled me in the dust ... My splendor is gone ..."

While Lamentations is a funeral song for the city of Jerusalem, these phrases might speak to the afflictions of chronic illness in marriages as well. The Israelites were experiencing brutal captivity by a powerful army, but God was still present with them. Compassionate. Faithful. And at work.

That is where the prayer of *Examen* begins.

5. Read the words of **Jeremiah 29:12-14:**

"Then you will call upon me and come and pray to me, and I will listen to you. You will seek me and find me when you seek me with all your heart. I will be found by you," declares the Lord, "and will bring you back from captivity. I will gather you from all the nations and places where I have banished you," declares the Lord, "and will bring you back to the place from which I carried you into exile."

In times of deep trouble, it may *seem* as though God has forgotten us. But He has not. He may instead be *preparing* us for a new beginning.

Have you experienced this kind of rebirth? New growth rising from deep hurt? Hope in the midst pain?

6. Read **John 6:44** and fill in the blanks:

_____ _____ can come to _____ unless

the _____ who _____ me _____ him,

and _____ will _____ him up at the

_____ day.

God is continually drawing us to Himself in and through Jesus, inviting us into a deeper relationship, a more intimate awareness of His presence and His voice in the everyday moments of our lives.

How could *Examen* change your relationship with your spouse? Use the **Journal Pages** at the end of this chapter to explore your response.

GOING DEEPER:

7. Now it's time to practice the prayer of *Examen*. Set aside 10-15 minutes in a quiet, comfortable place. Relax. Take a few deep, calming breaths and come before God in prayer.

    RECALL: In the past 24 hours:
    - Who or what are you most thankful for?
    - Who or what are you least thankful for?
    - When did you show God's love to others?
    - When did others show God's love to you?
    - What caused anger or frustration?
    - Where did you feel joy?
    - What scared you or caused you pain?
    - When were you at peace?
    - What caused you stress?
    - What made you sad?
    - When did you sense God's Presence?
    - When did God feel absent?
    - When did you move toward God?
    - When did you move away from God?
    - How did God speak to you?
    - When did He seem silent?

8. **RESPOND**
    - Is there something specific God is speaking to you today?
    - Is there a moment God is inviting you into more fully?
    - Where do you sense a deeper awareness of His presence in His Word, His creation, His people?
    - What do you need to lay down, surrender, or release?

9. **LOOK FORWARD**
    - What does your next 24 hours look like?
    - Will you face something unsettling or stressful?
    - Is there something that might cause you anxiety or fear?

- Where are you procrastinating?
- Is there something you can't wait to experience?
- What do you *feel* God saying to you?

Entering into Examen can feel vulnerable, but writing what you hear God speak in the stillness of your heart can become both life giving and faith building.

Start small. You don't have to show these words to anyone. They are just between you and God.

PRESSING ON:

10. How does the prayer *of Examen* apply to marriage?

    Read **Philippians 3:12-14** and fill in the blanks:

    _____ that I have _____ _____ all this, or have already been made _____, but I _____ _____ to _____ _____ of that for which _____ _____ took hold of _____. Brothers, I do not consider myself yet to have taken hold of it. But _____ _____ I do: _____ what is _____ and _____ toward that is _____, I _____ _____ toward the _____ to win the prize for which _____ has _____ me _____ in Christ Jesus.

The prayer of *Examen:*
- Cultivates an environment of love
- Reminds us to be humble and kind
- To be respectful
- To listen from the heart
- To be speak the truth in love
- To be part of a growing community
- To think the best about our spouse

Because those are the things we each long for ourselves.

PRAYER:

Dear Lord, we come to You at this moment right here and now to ask you to show us how to be present in each moment of every day and how to invite You into those moments. We know in our hearts our desire and deep need for You, yet we get so easily distracted by our own pain, worry, doubts and the fear. Show us how, with the help of the Holy Spirit, to invite You in at *all* times, as we seek to do Your will and thank you the many blessings in our lives. Amen.

Presence Journal

Presence Journal

Examen Journal

Examen Journal

[Love] does not dishonor others...
1 Corinthians 13:5a

Impact 9

I woke to quiet voices in the kitchen. My husband and middle daughter were heading out for an early morning walk and I sent them off with a kiss. They returned as I was finishing up my morning exercises, and Anna poked her head through my bedroom door. "How was your walk?" I asked. She smiled, shrugged, and headed silently back to the kitchen. "That's odd," I thought. It was uncharacteristic for my middle daughter to say nothing, and even odder for her to walk away quietly. She is joyful child, blessed with a lively, vibrant personality, and she generally lives life at both breakneck speed and full volume.

Minutes later I joined my husband at the breakfast table. I bowed my head and waited ... and waited ... *and waited*. I finally opened one eye, and discovered my husband already praying, not only silently, but *alone*.

"What on earth?" I wondered, a little frustrated. We pray together, *aloud*, and hand in hand whenever we can.

"Alrighty then," I thought, "I guess I'll pray alone. Father, thank you for this gorgeous morning, for the gift of another day with my husband and my kids. Help me to live for Your glory today, and Your glory alone. Flood my heart with peace and grant patience with my husband and my daughter. Their silence is starting to frustrate me. Amen."

As I ate, I noticed Anna occasionally glancing at my husband. Unexpectedly, she caught his eye and they both erupted into laughter, delighted, and finally revealing their secret. During their morning walk, they'd begun to wonder just how long it would take me to say something if they remained absolutely silent.

"Oh," I chuckled, "well, that explains everything."

I'd misread their silence, wondering if my husband was upset with me. I'd allowed their uncharacteristic behavior to seep into my attitude and sow seeds of irritation. And it caused me to wonder how often I mistakenly jump to the wrong conclusions, misunderstanding someone's words or misreading their actions because I know so few of their circumstances, so little of their situation.

James 4:12b reminds us, "But you, who are you to judge your neighbor?"

Who am I, indeed!

"Forgive me, Lord, for relying on my own finite, human vision and for allowing unexpected actions to affect my attitude. Thank you for the gentle lesson of an oddly unexpected silence to remind me that it's only as I rely on You moment by moment and day by day, that I will begin to see what is good and right and true. Amen."

I TAKE YOU IN SICKNESS & IN HEALTH | 111

STEPPING IN:

1. Read **Colossians 1:10-12** and fill in the blanks:

    And we _____ this in order that _____ may live a _____ _____ of the Lord and may _____ _____ in _____ way: bearing _____ in every _____ work, _____ in the _____ of _____, being _____ with all _____ according to his _____ _____ so that you may have great _____ and _____, and _____ giving _____ to the _____, who has _____ _____ to share in the _____ of the _____ in the _____ of _____.

    Whew! We could probably stop right there. So let's unpack these three verses a bit.

    First, Paul was writing to the believers in Colossae, a trading center about 100 miles east of Ephesus on the Lycus River, important not only as a crossroads for trade, but also for ideas. Paul had never met the Colossians, but he prayed for them faithfully.

2. What is the first thing Paul prays for in **verse 10**?

   What does it mean to live a life worthy of the Lord?

3. What is the second thing Paul asks for in **verse 10**?

   Is it possible to please God in every way?

4. What does it mean to bear fruit in every good work?

Read **Galatians 5:22**. What is the fruit of the Spirit?

-
-
-
-
-
-
-
-

5. What are the last seven words of **Galatians 5:22**?

6. The fruit of the Spirit is a gift, the spontaneous work of the Holy Spirit in us. On our own, we cannot produce this fruit. We can try. There are books, blogs, seminars, podcasts, classes, and retreats to help us grow these characteristics in our lives, but there is only one way this fruit matures and blossoms.

John 15:1, 2, 5 tells us how:

"_____ am the _____ vine, and my _____ is the _____. He _____ _____ every branch _____ me that _____ _____ fruit, while _____ branch that does _____ fruit he _____ so that it will be even _____ _____ ... I am the _____; _____ are the _____. If a man _____ in me and _____ in _____, he will bear _____ _____; _____ from _____ you can do _____."

The fruit of the Spirit — love, joy, peace, patience, kindness, goodness, faithfulness, gentleness and self-control — is a gift, the work of God's Spirit in us, possible only as we remain in Christ, and are shaped and pruned by God.

GOING DEEPER:

7. Take a few minutes today, and in the **Journal Pages** at the end of this chapter, write about your marriage relationship in light of these verses. Here are some questions to think about:

   - Where do you see God at work?
   - Where do you feel called to surrender?
   - Where do you hear His still, small voice?
   - Where do you feel His joy?
   - Where have you been hurt?
   - Is the fruit of the Spirit evident in your marriage?
   - Are you personally bearing much fruit?

8. Let's step back a few pages to **Colossians 1:10b–11**:

   "... growing in the knowledge of God, being strengthened with all power according to his glorious might so that you may have great endurance and patience, and joyfully giving thanks to the Father ..."

Continue on in the **Journal Pages** as you think about your marriage through the lens of **Colossians 1:10b–11**.

- Do you feel strengthened with all power?

- What would it mean to have great endurance and patience?

- What would it look like to joyfully give thanks to the Father?

Pleasant words are a honeycomb, sweet to the soul and healing to the bones.
Proverbs 16:24

9. Let's wrap it up with **Colossians 1:12b**:

"… giving thanks to the Father, who has qualified you to share in the inheritance of the saints in the kingdom of light."

Do you *feel* qualified?

Sit with that question for a while today. Give it some time to steep. When you're ready, read it again slowly. Read it aloud. Then write whatever God lays on your heart in the **Journal Pages** at the end of this chapter.

PRESSING ON:

10. Read **Philippians 3:15** and fill in the blanks:

    All of us who are _____ should take such a view of things. And if on _____ _____ you think _____, that _____ _____ will make _____ to _____.

    What if, held in the long view of eternity, we trusted God with our differing opinions too?

PRAYER:

Dear Father, too often we are quick to judge another. As **Matthew 7:3** so plainly points out, "Why do you look at the speck of sawdust in your brother's eye and pay no attention to the plank in your own eye?" Teach us instead to see others first with compassion, grace and mercy as You see us. Let us recognize how damaging and hurtful our judging words can be to those close to us and replace it with Your love so we may be an encouragement and a help and ultimately glorify You. Amen.

Impact Journal

Impact Journal

Love never fails.
1 Corinthians 13:8

Wellspring 10

Before sunrise, while the moon still lingered in the sky, I carried a surprise breakfast basket across the court and placed it beneath our neighbors' mailbox. It was the dawn of their 50th anniversary, a day deserving of celebration from its first waking moment to its final sleepy breath, and it reminded me of another morning years earlier.

That cold, January day, my then boyfriend Tony and I were headed north for a ski weekend. We stopped along the way at a small bakery, where we'd stopped months before. On our first visit, we'd waited in line behind an older couple. Gently, the man had reached for his wife's hand and said, "After fifty years of marriage, I still look forward to being with you every day."

"Wow," I thought. "Fifty years. That's a lifetime." I wondered not only what had sustained just this couple's marriage, but also their evident love for one another through fifty years of marriage.

Months later, as I stepped out of the car on an icy January morning, I remembered those tenderly spoken words and wondered if I'd ever love that deeply, if I'd ever be loved that deeply. Then Tony opened the bakery door, and I froze, for right there in the center of the glass case stood a cake frosted with the words, "Cindee, will you marry me?"

Touched by the memory of the older gentleman's words, Tony had chosen *this* place and *this* moment to propose. He grinned as dozens of people — employees, town residents, even the local newspaper photographer — poured from the bakery's back room, while I stood mute and amazed, trying to take it all in.

"Well," someone finally prompted, "are you going to marry him?"

I laughed through tears and simply nodded yes.

Without God, our marriage might have survived, but we'd have missed out on a love deeper, richer and more beautiful than we ever dreamed possible —love for a lifetime built on the bedrock of Jesus.

STEPPING IN:

1. Read **Galatians 6:9** and fill in the blanks:

   Let us not _____ _____ in doing good, for at the _____ _____ we will _____ a _____ if we _____ _____ _____ _____.

   The NASB version says: Let us not *lose heart* in doing good, for in due time we *will reap* if we do not grow weary (italics mine).

2. Read **2 Corinthians 4:1** and fill in the blanks:

   Therefore, since through _____ _____ we have this _____, we _____ _____ _____ _____.

   Have you ever thought of your marriage as a ministry?

What does the word ministry mean to you?

How would you define it?

3. **Matthew 20:28** says: "... the Son of Man did not come to be served, but to serve..." If that is true of Jesus, is it any less true of us?

   What might change if we began to look for ways to serve our spouses? Not out of obligation, but from a wellspring of love? Explore this idea in the **Journal Pages** at the end of this chapter.

4. Read **1 Peter 4:10** and fill in the blanks:

   Each one should use whatever _____ he has _____ to _____ _____, _____ administering _____ _____ in its _____ forms.

I TAKE YOU IN SICKNESS & IN HEALTH

What gifts has God given you?

We're going to go a little "off script" here and do some brainstorming, something a little bit different than discussing spiritual gifts. We're going to look at the specific ways God has poured His creativity into you.

Turn to the **Journal Pages** at the end of this chapter and begin to make a list of all those things that make your heart sing. For example:
- music
- the scent of lilacs
- freshly baked bread
- watching ocean waves crash and roll
- candlelight,
- firelight
- the feel of your favorite pillow

Now think about your spouse. What makes your spouse's heart sing? List as many as you can.

Chose one and circle it. This week, how can you offer this gift to your spouse? Is it something you can do together, like enjoy his favorite meal or join her at her favorite coffee shop? Is it a small gift you can give, such as time together or flowers in a vase on the table?

If you have trouble with this exercise, that's OK. Change is difficult. And sacrifice always comes with a cost.

5. Read **John 15:13** and fill in the blanks:

   Greater _____ has no one than this, that he _____ _____ his _____ for his _____.

   Sacrifice costs, because it calls us to something greater. It calls us to love like Jesus.

6. Read **John 13:34** and fill in the blanks:

   A _____ _____ I give you: _____ _____ _____. As _____ have loved _____, so _____ must _____ _____ _____.

   The day my husband and I walked down the aisle, all those present could *see* the love we had for one another. Our love was conspicuous and celebrated.

   Conspicuous love is clear, apparent and significant. Conspicuous love is reassuring, unmistakable, unconditional and undeniable.

   And conspicuous love requires sacrifice, effort and commitment.

I TAKE YOU IN SICKNESS & IN HEALTH

GOING DEEPER:

7. Read **Ephesians 5:1-2** and fill in the blanks:

   Be _____ of _____, therefore, as _____ loved children and _____ a _____ of _____, just as Christ _____ offering and _____ to _____.

   This is a tough verse to read if your marriage is in crisis, and chronic illness can spin even a strong marriage into crisis. Yet as long as there is breath, there is hope. God *can* redeem the "years the locusts have eaten." (**Joel 2:25**)

   But redemption comes with a cost — the commitment of sacrificial love.

8. Read **Isaiah 44:22** and fill in the blanks:

   I have _____ away your _____ like a _____, your _____ like the _____. _____ to me, for _____ have _____ you.

   This is God's redemptive love for us. Arms wide open. Sins swept away.

9. What would redemptive love look like for your marriage? Spend some time over the next few days in prayer. Then when you're ready, write those thoughts on the special **Redemptive Love Journal Pages** at the end of this chapter.

PRESSING ON:

10. We've been working our way through **1 Corinthians 13:4-8a and 13** in this study. 1 Corinthians 13 is often called the love chapter. Read those verses now and fill in the blanks:

   And now I will show you the most excellent way …

   Love is _____, love is _____. It does _____ _____, it does _____ _____, it is _____ _____. It is _____ _____, it is _____ _____, it is _____ easily _____, it keeps _____ record of _____. Love does _____ delight in evil but _____ with the _____. It always _____, always _____, always _____, always _____. _____ _____ _____.

   And now these _____ remain: _____, _____ and _____. But the _____ of these is _____.

   God's redeeming love for you and your spouse flows *with*, *in* and *through* Christ.

Has the Lord redeemed you? Then speak it out! Psalm 107:2 NLT

Let those who have been redeemed by the Lord declare it ... Psalm 107:2 ISV

Beloved, let us love one another, for love is from God, and whoever loves has been born of God and knows God. 1 John 4:7 NIV

God has shown you the most excellent way ... 1 Corinthians 13:1

PRAYER:

Father of all creation, we come to You this day seeking Your guidance and direction in our lives. Help us to see beyond our limited capacity to understand. Show us how we can serve with kindness and tenderness so the words we speak are an encouragement and a help to all who are in need, and especially our spouse. Allow us to once again see love and the beautiful gift of marriage as You intended. Amen.

Wellspring Journal

Wellspring Journal

Redemptive Love Journal

Redemptive Love Journal

Two are better than one, because they have a good return for their labor: If either of them falls down, one can help the other up...if two lie down together, they will keep warm... A cord of three strands is not quickly broken.
Ecclesiastes 4:9-11, 12b

Appendix

Small Group Policy

AS A GROUP, WE WILL:
- Create a space where people feel cared for, prayed for, encouraged and respected — a place people can't wait to return to!
- Limit the group size to six people or fewer to allow each person the opportunity to participate without feeling rushed.
- Recognize that there will be ups and downs and that pain and illness will sometimes cause us to speak or respond in uncharacteristic ways.
- Start and end on time, respecting the energy limits of each member.
- Be open and authentic, creating the opportunity for deeper relationships with each other and with God.
- Engage in discussion, allowing each member a chance to speak and be heard.
- Affirm and respond when someone shares. Vulnerability is risky. Encourage one another.
- Keep what is said here private and confidential.
- Be gracious and kind. We're each affected differently by illness, we're each at a different point in the journey and we may not share the same views on healing, medications, diets, treatments or doctors.
- Let the facilitator know if you won't be there and how the group can pray for you.
- Be considerate of the needs of others by:
  - not wearing perfume, cologne or scented lotions.
  - not soliciting the sale of products or services.
  - offering group members the freedom to sit, stand and move to increase comfort.

SIGN: _____

DATE: _____

Small Group Contact Information

Name:
Address:
Email:
Phone:

Name:
Address:
Email:
Phone:

Name:
Address:
Email:
Phone:

Name:
Address:
Email:
Phone:

Name:
Address:
Email:
Phone:

Name:
Address:
Email:
Phone:

*Above all, love each other deeply,
because love covers over
a multitude of sins.*
1 Peter 4:8

Build an Illness Ministry

STEPPING IN:

WHY DO WE NEED A CHRONIC ILLNESS MINISTRY?

1. Approximately *1 in 2 people* live with one or more chronic illnesses.
2. Mental illness affects *1 in 5 adults*.
3. Many with chronic illness are hurting, lonely and exhausted.
4. Many struggle with anxiety, depression, pain and/or significant limitations.
5. Many with chronic illness don't look sick, so they become an invisible statistic.
6. Chronic illness can be a staggering financial burden. According to the CDC, 86% of all health care spending in 2010 was for people with chronic medical conditions.
7. Chronic illness affects marriage, family, faith, finances, friendships, education, hobbies, and work — in short, every aspect of life.

WHAT CAN YOU DO?

1. Start the conversation. Begin with one person you know who has chronic illness. Ask them what it's like. Listen. Try to hear what they might not be saying.
2. Invite a small group to brainstorm about what a chronic illness ministry might look like in your church, neighborhood, workplace or organization. Might it include awareness? Resources? Education? A small group? Counseling? Transportation? Meals? Financial assistance?

3. Think about possible service projects. How could this ministry offer opportunities for participants to *invest in others*?
4. Could you offer a Bible study? How often? How long?
5. Think about caregivers. What could you do to help them?

GOING DEEPER:

ONCE YOU'VE DECIDED TO START A MINISTRY

1. **Create a Mission Statement**
   Example: To provide a safe, caring, loving environment in which people can grieve, accept, and learn to thrive in a life with chronic illness.

2. **Develop a Vision Statement**
   Example: To facilitate participation between those living with chronic illness and [your organization] — an opportunity to serve and minister to those with chronic illness, including them as vital, necessary and important members, and offering them creative opportunities to serve and be involved.

3. **Small Groups**
   - Consider these four core group values as you launch your first small group: *Hope, Purpose, Worth, Joy* and how these values connect us deeply to God and to one another, how they help us connect, grow and serve right where we are.
   - We suggest biweekly meetings of 90 minutes or less.
   - Small groups of up to six participants each are recommended to allow each person the opportunity to share and be heard.
   - Consider starting a virtual group using Facebook video, Skype or Google Hangouts.
   - Consider the needs of your participants:
     - access to bathrooms
     - space for those who may need to sit, stand, or walk a bit to be comfortable
     - perhaps a few high tables for those who may need to stand
     - wheelchair accessibility
     - time of day and day of week

- food restrictions if you offer refreshments
- cost to participants

4. **Caregivers**

   Caregivers need care too. Consider hosting a group specifically for them.

5. **Resources**

   What will you need to facilitate this ministry?
   - A place to meet?
   - Printed materials?
   - Curricula?
   - Financial support?
   - The support of a pastor or trained counselor?
   - Email, website, database and/or social media support?
   - Refreshments?

6. **Curricula**
   - The Chronic Joy Thrive Series — *Discovering Hope, Finding Purpose, Embracing Worth* and *Encountering Joy* — are specifically designed for chronic illness small groups.

7. **Leaders**
   - Who will lead small groups and for how long?
   - Will you provide training for them?
   - A wealth of resources to equip small group leaders is available at **www.chronic-joy.org**.

PRESSING ON:

8. **Service Opportunities**

   How can those in your chronic illness small groups begin to serve others in your church, organization, community or around the world? Here's a short list to get you thinking.

- Write cards or letters for those who are hospitalized or homebound.
- Write to soldiers or missionaries serving overseas.
- Make colorful cards for children's meal trays at your local children's hospital.
- Read to a child or for the visually impaired.
- Knit or crochet prayer shawls, baby blankets, mittens, hats or scarves for those who are grieving, facing surgery or in homeless shelters.
- Bake cookies for a youth event, bake sale or for someone who is homebound.
- Send birthday cards to nursing home residents.
- Make "care kits" with shampoo, soap, toothbrushes, deodorant, healthy snacks, etc., to donate to the homeless/homeless shelters.
- Make hospital care bags for those in the hospital or their caregivers — healthy snacks, fruit, homemade cookies or breads, a soft blanket, toothpaste, lotion, a book, puzzle or game, gift cards for gas, the hospital cafeteria, toiletries, etc.
- Create "Birthday in a Bag" kits for local children's shelters. Include party hats, plates, cups, napkins, forks, a cake mix, frosting, candles, etc.

Be creative. Look for opportunities. Brainstorm ideas. Serving unlocks the door to hope.

Reproducible Prayer Card

⚭ Prayer

"For where two or three are gathered together in my name, there am I in the midst of them." Matthew 18:20

How you can pray for me this week:
_____
_____

Where I experienced hope this week:
_____
_____

NIV Scripture Used in the Study

CHAPTER 1

Question 5:　**1 Corinthians 13:2b-3**
… and if I have a faith that can move mountains, but have not love, I am nothing. If I give all I possess to the poor and surrender my body to the flames, but have not love, I gain nothing.

Question 9:　**1 Corinthians 13:4a**
Love is patient, love is kind.

CHAPTER 2

Question 7:　**Matthew 17:20b-21**
I tell you the truth, if you have faith as small as a mustard seed, you can say to this mountain, "Move from here to there" and it will move. Nothing will be impossible for you.

CHAPTER 3

Question 1:　**1 Kings 8:56a**
Praise be to the Lord, who has given rest to his people …

Question 2:　**1 Kings 8:57a**
May the Lord our God be with us …

Question 3:　**1 Kings 8:57b**
May he never leave us nor forsake us …

Question 4:　**1 Kings 8:58** and fill in the blanks:
May he turn our hearts to him, to walk in all his ways …

Question 5: **1 Kings 8:59a, 60a**
And may these words of mine, which I have prayed before the Lord, be near to the Lord our God day and night, that he may uphold the cause of his servant and the cause of his people Israel according to each day's need ...

Question 6: **1 Kings 8:60**
... so that all the peoples of the earth may know that the Lord is God and that there is no other.

Question 7: **1 Kings 8:56-60**
Praise be to the Lord, who has given rest to his people Israel just as he promised. Not one word has failed of all the good promises he gave through his servant Moses. May the Lord our God be with us as he was with our fathers; may he never leave us nor forsake us. May he turn our hearts to him, to walk in all his ways and to keep the commands, decrees and regulations he gave our fathers. And may these words of mine, which I have prayed before the Lord, be near to the Lord our God day and night, that he may uphold the cause of his servant and the cause of his people Israel according to each day's need, so that all the peoples of the earth may know that the Lord is God and that there is no other.

Question 10: **1 Corinthians 13:4**
Love is patient, love is kind. It does not envy, it does not boast, it is not proud.

CHAPTER 4

Question 1: **1 Corinthians 13:5b-c**
... it is not self-seeking, it is not easily angered ...

Question 6: **Psalm 103:11-12**
For as high as the heavens are above the earth, so great is his love for those who fear him; as far as the east is from the west, so far has he removed our transgressions from us.

Question 7:   **Psalm 103:8**
               The Lord is compassionate and gracious, slow to anger, abounding in love.

Question 8:   **Psalm 103:8d**
               … abounding in love.

Question 10:   **Luke 23:34**
               Jesus said, "Father, forgive them, for they do not know what they are doing."

               Ephesians 2:10
               For we are God's workmanship, created in Christ Jesus to do good works, which God prepared in advance for us to do.

CHAPTER 5

Question 1:   **Psalm 90:12**
               Teach us to number our days aright, that we may gain a heart of wisdom.

Question 2:   **Ephesians 5:15-16a**
               Be very careful, then, how you live — not as unwise but as wise, making the most of every opportunity …

Question 5:   **Psalm 39:5**
               You have made my days a mere handbreadth; the span of my years is as nothing before you. Each man's life is but a breath.

               Psalm 39:11b
               … each man's life is but a breath.

Question 6:   **Psalm 40:17b**
               You are my help and my deliverer; O my God, do not delay.

Matthew 25:35-36

For I was hungry and you gave me something to eat, I was thirsty and you gave me something to drink, I was a stranger and you invited me in, I needed clothes and you clothed me, I was sick and you looked after me, I was in prison and you came to visit me.

Question 9: **James 4:14**

Why you do not even know what will happen tomorrow. What is your life? You are a mist that appears for a little while and then vanishes. Instead, you ought to say, "If it is the Lord's will, we will live and do this or that."

CHAPTER 6

Question 1: **Genesis 2:20**

So the man gave names to all the livestock, the birds of the air and all the beasts of the field. But for Adam no suitable helper was found.

Question 2: **Genesis 2:21-22**

So the Lord God caused the man to fall into a deep sleep; and while he was sleeping, he took one of the man's ribs and closed up the place with flesh. Then the Lord God made a woman from the rib he had taken out of the man, and he brought her to the man.

Genesis 2:23

The man said, "This is now bone of my bones and flesh of my flesh; she shall be called 'woman,' for she was taken out of man."

Question 6: **Song of Solomon 1:2**

Let him kiss me with the kisses of his mouth — for your love is more delightful than wine.

Question 7: **Song of Solomon 1:15a**
How beautiful you are, my darling! Oh, how beautiful!

Song of Solomon 1:16a
How handsome you are, my lover! Oh, how charming!

Question 8: **Song of Solomon 1:6**
Do not stare at me because I am dark, because I am darkened by the sun.

Question 9: **Song of Solomon 2:3**
Like an apple tree among the trees of the forest is my lover among the young men.

Question 10: **Song of Solomon 3:11**
Come out, you daughters of Zion, and look at King Solomon wearing the crown with which him mother crowned him on the day of his wedding, the day his heart rejoiced.

CHAPTER 7

Question 1: **Proverbs 27:17**
As iron sharpens iron, so one man sharpens another.

Question 2: **Romans 15:5-6**
May the God who gives endurance and encouragement give you a spirit of unity among yourselves as you follow Christ Jesus, so that with one heart and mouth you may glorify the God and Father of our Lord Jesus Christ.

Question 4: **Ephesians 3:14-20**
For this reason I kneel before the Father, from whom his whole family in heaven and on earth derives its name. I pray that out of his glorious riches he may strengthen you with power through his Spirit in your inner being, so that Christ may dwell in your hearts through faith. And I pray that you, being rooted and established in love, may have power

together with all the saints, to grasp how wide and long and high and deep is the love of Christ, and to know this love that surpasses knowledge — that you may be filled to the measure of all the fullness of God. Now to him who is able to do immeasurably more than all we ask or imagine, according to his power that is at work within us, to him be glory in the church and in Christ Jesus throughout all generations, for ever and ever! Amen.

Question 5: **Proverbs 3:5-6**
Trust in the Lord with all your heart and lean not on your own understanding; in all your ways acknowledge him, and he will make your paths straight.

Question 6: **Colossians 3:12-14**
Therefore, as God's chosen people, holy and dearly loved, clothe yourselves with compassion, kindness, humility, gentleness and patience. Bear with each other and forgive whatever grievances you may have against one another. Forgive as the Lord forgave you. And over all these virtues put on love, which binds them all together in perfect unity.

Question 9: **Galatians 6:10a**
Therefore, as we have opportunity, let us do good to all people ...

CHAPTER 8

Question 1: **Lamentations 3:19-26**
I remember my affliction and my wandering, the bitterness and the gall. I well remember them, and my soul is downcast within me. Yet this I call to mind and therefore I have hope: Because of the Lord's great love we are not consumed, for His compassions never fail. They are new every morning; Great is your faithfulness. I say to myself, "The Lord is my portion; therefore I will wait for him." The Lord is good to those whose hope is in him, to the one who

seeks him; it is good to wait quietly for salvation of the Lord.

Question 3: **Lamentations 3:1a**
I am the man who has seen affliction ...

Question 4: **Jeremiah 29:12-14**
"Then you will call upon me and come and pray to me, and I will listen to you. You will seek me and find me when you seek me with all your heart. I will be found by you," declares the Lord, "and will bring you back from captivity. I will gather you from all the nations and laces where I have banished you," declares the Lord, "and will bring you back to the place from which I carried you into exile."

Question 5: **John 6:44**
"No one can come to me unless the Father who sent me draws him, and I will raise up at the last day ..."

Question 10: **Philippians 3:12-14**
I know what it is to be in need, and I know what it is to have plenty. I have learned the secret of being content in any and every situation, whether well fed or hungry, whether living in plenty or in want. I can do everything through him who gives me strength. Yet it was good of you to share in my troubles.

CHAPTER 9

Question 1: **Colossians 1:10-12:**
And we pray this in order that you may live a life worthy of the Lord and may please him in every way: bearing fruit in every good work, growing in the knowledge of God, being strengthened with all power according to his glorious might so that you may have great endurance and patience, and joyfully giving thanks to the Father, who has qualified

you to share in the inheritance of the saints in the kingdom of light.

Question 4: **Galatians 5:22a**
But the fruit of the Spirit is love, joy, peace, patience, kindness, goodness, faithfulness, gentleness and self-control.

Question 6: **John 15:1, 2, 5**
"I am the true vine, and my Father is the gardener. He cuts off every branch in me that bears no fruit, while every branch that does bear fruit he prunes so that it will be even more fruitful ... I am the vine; you are the branches. If a man remains in me and I in him, he will bear much fruit; apart from me you can do nothing.

Question 8: **Colossians 1:10b-11**
"... growing in the knowledge of God, being strengthened with all power according to his glorious might so that you may have great endurance and patience, and joyfully giving thanks to the Father ..."

Proverbs 16:24
Pleasant words are a honeycomb, sweet to the soul and healing to the bones.

Question 9: **Colossians 1:12b**
... giving thanks to the Father, who has qualified you to share in the inheritance of the saints in the kingdom of light.

Question 10: **Philippians 3:15**
All of us who are mature should take such a view of things. And if on some point you think differently, that too God will make clear to you.

CHAPTER 10

Question 1: **Galatians 6:9**
Let us not become weary in doing good, for at the proper time we will reap a harvest if we do not give up.

Question 2: **2 Corinthians 4:1**
Therefore, since through God's mercy we have this ministry, we do not lose heart.

Question 3: **Matthew 20:28**
... the Son of Man did not come to be served, but to serve.

Question 4: **1 Peter 4:10**
Each one should use whatever gift he has received to serve others, faithfully administering God's grace in its various forms.

Question 5: **John 15:13**
Greater love has no one than this, that he lay down his life for his friends.

Question 6: **John 13:34**
A new command I give you: Love one another. As I have loved you, so you must love one another.

Question 7: **Ephesians 5:1-2**
Be imitators of God, therefore, as dearly loved children and live a life of love, just as Christ loved us and gave himself up for us as a fragrant offering and sacrifice to God.

Question 8: **Isaiah 44:22**
I have swept away your offenses like a cloud, your sins like the morning mist. Return to me, for I have redeemed you.

Question 10: **1 Corinthians 13:4-8a, 13**
Love is patient, love is kind. It does not envy, it does not boast, it is not proud. It is not rude, it is not self-seeking, it is not easily angered, it keeps no record of wrongs Love does not delight in evil but rejoices with the truth. It always protects, always trusts, always hopes, always perseveres. Love never fails ... And now these three remain: faith, hope and love. But the greatest of these is love.

Cindee Snider Re

Cindee is married to Tony, the man she loves most in this world. They are parents of five, ages 17-25. She and four of her five kids have Ehlers-Danlos, a genetic connective tissue disorder, and myriad co-existing conditions. While a life steeped in illness isn't what Cindee would have chosen, she also wouldn't have wanted to miss it, for she's learning that the deeper the valley, the greater her capacity for joy, for it's there, sewn into every hard, beautiful, precious moment.

Cindee is co-founder of Chronic Joy Ministry, Inc., author of the Chronic Joy Thrive Series and a passionate photographer. She and her family live in Sussex, Wisconsin, on an acre of towering pines, sugar maples and sprawling white oak that is also home to whitetail deer, wild turkey, red fox, sandhill cranes and a symphony of songbirds. Her passions include poetry, photography, research and tea. Luci Shaw is an all-time favorite poet, the Canon 100mm macro her favorite lens (though the 85mm f1.2 is a close second), and though she frequently forgets to eat, she is never without a cup, glass or bottle of her favorite Earl Grey tea. She also serves as a patient representative on several medical grant boards.

Cindee's writing inspires readers to dig deeper, lean harder and breathe deeply of God's amazing grace.

Author Photo: Courtesy of Babboni Photography

Acknowledgments

Thank you to the *I Take You in Sickness & in Health Feedback* Team: Diane & Sherm McElwain, Christine & Richard Feldschneider, Karin & Rick Fendick, Sandie Lovrein, Heidi & Jeff Peterson, Kris Hansson Robinson, and Gina & Randy Weeks for your thoughtful and encouraging feedback, questions and comments.

To my dear friend and ministry co-founder, **Pamela Piquette**, thank you for helping me carve out the time and space to write, and for encouraging me along the way.

Thank you to **Todd and Heather Johnson, Mike and Mary Juneau, Heidi Peterson, Eric and Jenni Steingraeber**, the Board of Chronic Joy Ministry. It is an honor to serve with you!

Thank you to **Sheila Lagrand**, my dear friend, who is intimately acquainted with this journey through chronic illness for writing the Foreword. I am so grateful!

To my parents, **Don and Susie Snider**, thank you for your legacy of more than 50 years of marriage. You have set the bar high, with you beautiful legacy of love.

Thank you to **Wayde Peronto** of **Babboni Photography** for the gift of my author photo, possible because of **Shelly Esser**'s four-page interview of Pamela and me for **Just Between Us Magazine**, Summer, 2017 edition.

To my husband, **Tony**, the man I love most in this world, thank you for loving me, believing in me, encouraging me, praying with me, *staying with me*, and generously supporting the mission and ministry of Chronic Joy. None of this would be possible without you. Thank you for writing the prayers for this book.

To my **Heavenly Father**, thank you for teaching me every day what it means to love.

To each person reading this book: I pray you will find God in these words and that through them you will grow stronger as a couple as you grow stronger *together* in Christ, discovering the *love of a lifetime*.

Discovering Hope

Beginning the Journey Toward Hope in Chronic Illness

Discovering Hope is an invitation to experience radical hope and compassionate change in a life with chronic illness. No matter how dark the days, how wild the storm, how deep the valley or how long the winter, there is hope.

There is always hope.

Discovering Hope is a powerful, practical, insightful and well-written guide for all those affected by chronic physical and mental illness.

Embrace a new perspective. Celebrate the small victories. Wrestle with difficult questions. And learn to laugh again. Often.

No matter what today looks like, there is hope.

Finding Purpose
Rediscovering Meaning in a Life with Chronic Illness

What if purpose looks different than we believe? What if purpose isn't defined by education, gifts or passion? Isn't determined by what we are able to do? Isn't affected by what we've lost due to chronic illness?

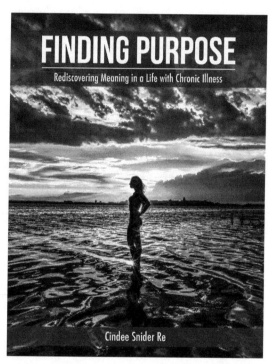

What if, instead, purpose simply aligns us with God? What if we are called *to be* instead of *to do?*

Finding Purpose is a 10-chapter study inviting participants to rethink their understanding of purpose, to release cultural definitions and to embrace God's — a definition both rooted in timeless biblical truths and as refreshing as a gentle spring rain.

Embracing Worth

Understanding Your Value in a Life with Chronic Illness

You are valued, sustained, beloved.

RELEASING IN 2018

Encountering Joy

Embracing God's Presence in a Life with Chronic Illness

RELEASING IN 2019

Grace, Truth & Time
Facilitating Small Groups That Thrive

This valuable guide is chock-full of resources designed to empower even the most hesitant leader to become a confident, thoughtful and well-prepared facilitator.

Learn to lead through God's grace; to create a space for spiritual growth and healing; to empathize, listen and engage with those in pain; to grow in prayer and compassion; to foster hope and encouragement; and to build thriving small group communities. If you've ever wondered or even doubted if you could lead a thriving chronic illness small group, this book is for you.

Connect

- chronic-joy.org
- cjministry
- chronicjoymin
- chronicjoy
- chronicjoyministry
- care@chronic-joy.org

WE VALUE YOUR FEEDBACK.

care@chronic-joy.org

Made in the USA
Lexington, KY
10 January 2019